Fragments: God Loves Everyone

Fragments: God Loves Everyone

(Sharing Jesus with My Generation)

Reflections on the Love, Teachings, and Commission of Christ

Samuel Agyeman Tabi

FRAGMENTS: GOD LOVES EVERYONE

Published by
CreateSpace
4900 LaCross Road,
North Charleston, SC 29406

ISBN 10: 1542924553
ISBN 13: 9781542924559
Library of Congress Control Number: 2017916009
CreateSpace Independent Publishing Platform
North Charleston, South Carolina
Unless otherwise stated, scripture quotations are taken from the Holy Bible, New International Version, copyright 1973 by the International Bible Society.

COVER DESIGN
Suona Multimedia
Creative Design Bureau
Via IV Novembre 121/A,
25080 Prevale – BS
DESIGNS@SUONAMULTIMEDIA.COM

Table of Contents

Foreword   ix

Acknowledgements   xi

Preface   xiii

Introduction   xv

Prologue   xvii

Main Scriptural Text   xxi

1   God Is Eager to Save   1

2   God Loves the World   6

3   The Father's Love   14

4   The Golden Rule   32

5   The New Birth   46

6   Missiological Insight   57

7   The Cynosure of the Gospel   68

8   The Essentiality of Jesus   76

9   God's Judgement   85

10   Heaven as a Promise   90

11   God Cares for You   94

Conclusion of *Fragments: God Loves Everyone.*   103

Prayer of salvation: 108

To all those who love our Lord Jesus Christ and all those who have not believed in Him.

Foreword

THIS BOOK IS a wholesome exploration of the love of God as described in the Bible. It systematically describes how God has shown His love to all through His Son, Jesus Christ. The author has made good use of current understanding of the Bible's truth and historic accounts to justify the application of God's word in people's lives.

This book will serve as a guide to the lost, stabilise the faith of the Christian believer, and motivate the Christian to spread the Gospel of Christ. It will provide spiritual food for the hungry and water for the thirsty. In this live-streaming account of God's love, readers will understand the depth of God's love through Christ and the subsequent provision of salvation to all.

The author has carefully identified the reality of God's love. He asserts that Jesus is the only way, the only truth, and the only life-giver. He reinforces the solution of humankind state in Christ. Christ the Messiah is the centre of the book, and I highly recommend it to everyone who needs to have a personal relationship with Him.

The book you now hold in your hands is carefully written and emphasises:

- God's love for humankind. This love is not limited to colour, age, gender, or social class. It is available to all, and those who accept His love and believe in His Son, Jesus Christ, are saved.

- Our purpose in sharing the love of God to all through extensive missiological pursuits.
- The need for Jesus in everyone's life.
- Issues related to life after death, judgement, rewards, and the need to be focused on heaven.

Fragments will inspire you to praise and worship God as you observe the unique presence of God in the affairs of people and appreciate the length, breadth, and width of the love of God for all. By this observation, you will be able to rest your hope in the Bible as the true word of God and worthy of obeying.

All will find this book a rich compendium of complementary biblical resources and will appreciate the incomprehensible depth of the nature of God's love.

I strongly recommend it to all.

Reverend Professor Kwabena Agyapong-Kodua
National Youth Pastor, the Church of Pentecost—UK

Acknowledgements

- The compilation of this book is the result of concerted efforts of friends and families without whose help this book would not have been published.

- A special thank-you and God's blessings to my parents, Apostle and Mrs. Agyeman Tabi, for bringing me into this world and training me in the fear of the Lord and standing by me when I was growing up.

- Grateful thanks to my sisters: Sarah, Stefania, and Anna, for continually supporting me and praying for me while I slaved away at this book. Thank-you to Kelvin Dickson for his "little" prayers.

- I am extremely grateful to my grandmother, Madam Comfort Abbrey, for reading the book and suggesting ideas. God bless you.

- A special thank-you to Samuel Asamoah, my uncle and Elder of the Church of Pentecost in Dallas, Texas, for his love and support. God bless you and your family.

- A special thank-you and God's blessings to John William Ahwireng, B.A. (Languages), M.A. (Comparative Literature), PhD (ongoing), Diploma in Journalism, for his careful editing and suggestions to keep going.

- I would like to show my grateful feeling to Apostle Professor Opoku Onyinah, chairman of the Church of Pentecost, for endorsing the book; to Apostle Dr. Alfred Koduah of the Church of Pentecost, for the hour phone discussion we had concerning this book.

- I express my deepest thanks and God's blessings to Apostle Newton Ofosuhene Nyarko, national head of the Church of Pentecost in Italy, for introducing me to Reverend Professor Kwabena Agyapong-Kodua. Thank-you to Professor for writing the Foreword of this book.

- It is my radiant sentiment to place on record my deepest gratitude to Apostle Dr. Raymond K. Akam and Apostle Kojo Adu Yeboah for their endorsements.

- Thank-you to Elder Frank Frimpong, chairman of the Literature Committee of the Church of Pentecost, Italy, for reading the manuscript and suggesting ideas.

- Thank-you to all friends for your time and kind words.

Preface

I WAS BLESSED to be raised in a Christian family. My parents are born-again Christians and, at the same time, gospel preachers. Currently, my parents are in Vienna, Austria, as missionaries.

At the age of 14, on the 23rd of June 2000, I gave my life to Christ as my personal Lord and Saviour and was baptised on the same day, in a stream called Bobo, in the Ashanti Region of Ghana.

After I had believed in Christ, the passion to share the Gospel of Christ became part of my life and the words of the Great Commission "Go into the world and preach the gospel" (Matthew 28:18–20) reverberated in me for days, months, and years. I just couldn't get away from the words of the Great Commission. Honestly, the words are still reverberating in me. I had a strange feeling that I would be a good vessel for God's kingdom to lead others to Christ.

A sense of urgency seemed to descend upon me, arising, I thought from the fact that having now been in Christ and in Christianity for almost two decades, and not just believing in Christ, but also walking with Him and being faithful in my service to Him as my Lord and King, it dawned on me to be obedient and also to preach the gospel and disciple others for Christ.

One day I decided to write a book about Jesus. Taking my pen and notepad, I began to scribble some thoughts. I reflected on the fact that Jesus died for the sins of the world, including me! Now I have been saved by the grace of God but there are still others who are yet to come to Christ. And since salvation is for everyone, I decided to write a book on the subject "God loves everyone" in fragments.

Finally, as I allowed my mind to run over, I decided to title the book, *Fragments: God Loves Everyone*. God loves you. God loves me. God loves everyone. For this reason, God sent His son Jesus to die for us.

God bless you.

Introduction

A REPUTABLE INTERNATIONAL Christian association, the Gideon's International, tasked with the purpose of promoting the Gospel of Christ to all people worldwide, has this to say about the Bible: It "contains the mind of God, the state of man, the way of salvation, the doom of sinners and the happiness of believers." The Gideon's International goes on to add that "the Bible is the traveller's map, the pilgrim's staff, the pilot's compass, the soldier's sword and the Christian charter." In the last part of the Bible, the association says that "Paradise is restored, Heaven is opened, and the gates of hell disclosed. Christ, obviously is the grand subject and the greatest personality who assures the way to heaven."

Why then do you delay reading the Bible daily? Studying the Bible cannot be done within a short period of time. And that's why this treasure of the holy book should be studied in bits, if not, in fragments. Therefore, a fragmentary study of the Bible leads to the idea to name this book *Fragments: God Loves Everyone*.

Fragments could well be read as a critical exploration of the Bible concepts capable of shaping the Christian way of life. Moral lessons that abound would help and add more values and virtues to the Christian who reads the biblical messages.

Read *Fragments* "to be wise." This book contains light to direct you, food to nourish you, and comfort to cheer you.

In each of the chapters, you will discover that Jesus, being the best, died to save humankind from perishing. This is because God's love is unexplainable. Jonah proved to be recalcitrant to God, but in the end, he was saved. The prodigal son's elder brother was filled with jealousy towards his own brother, instead of being happy for his repentance and coming back to his father.

Are you afraid that you are a sinner and God will not rescue you from perishing? Come to Jesus the Saviour, no matter the magnitude of your sins. Jesus has the best panacea for all your numerous problems. There are also additional benefits when you come to Jesus and make Him your Lord and Saviour, such as eternal life, God being your heavenly Father, and becoming a member in God's Kingdom.

Read *Fragments* to encourage you to come to Doctor Jesus. It is hoped that readers, and for that matter, Christians, will benefit immensely upon reading this book, and all your thoughts will vapourise into thin air.

Prologue

FRAGMENTS CONTAINS RELIGIOUS model framework in series aimed at giving alertness to humanity about impending doom awaiting for them should they remain in their sinful nature. Christians are admonished that the end time is near, and there is the need to repent from their sins and follow the precepts, statutes and commandments of God. Through these fragmental teachings of God, it is clear that Our Merciful God, is fully committed to forgive any human being their sins irrespective of the magnitude of such a sin.

The wages of sin, as it is always said is death. God does not want any sinner to perish, hence He sends His agents to send the Messages abroad. Similarly, God is eager and desirous to save human beings from a lake of fire that has been prepared for Satan and his angels. Consequently, God invites His creatures for total transformation of life – repentance which is a prerequisite to earn eternal salvation.

As we live in a world of turbulence and lawlessness, and humanity perverts ruthlessly His laws, God would send His messengers to warn His people to desist from their sinfulness in order to avoid destruction.

God being merciful and eager to save, sends Jonah to warn the inhabitants of Nineveh about their destruction. Having heeded to the warning from God, the people of Nineveh changed and repented; and they are saved. The messenger Jonah initially refused to carry God's message to the people of Nineveh and was thrown into the sea. God saved him after He (God) had prepared a fish to swallow Jonah lying in the belly of the fish for three days. What a rescue!

God does not want any person to perish. As a spiritual being, He sends His only begotten Son Jesus to come to the world to manifest God's character to humanity. As sin has created a gulf between creatures and the Creator, His Son made atonement as His blood is used to cleanse our sins. The only thing we should hold forth is that we should have faith in Jesus, for He is the path to righteousness and to God.

Jesus came to the world to show the love of God to humanity. While on earth as an ambassador of God, He did a lot of things for mankind. He healed the sick and taught men about the Kingdom of God. Jesus, before He ascended into heaven, gave us the work of the Great Commission (See Matthew 28:19–20). How far have you done your part of that work?

Despite some Christian's refusal to spread the gospel abroad, God continues to care for us. God has to let His church, His people, to reach out and spread the gospel to the entire world. It's what we have been called to do. Spreading the truth about Jesus and what He has done for us (John 3:16), what He is doing now for us (Romans 8:34) and what He will do for us in the future (1 Thessalonians 4:16) is truly our mission. Mission is a core part of God's sovereign activity in the process of redeeming humanity. Many missionary activities are recorded in the Bible and Master Jesus is in one of them.

In the end, the Christian mission is not ours; it originated in the heart of God; it is based on the love of God; and it is accomplished by the will of God. As Christ's ambassadors, we are called to a comprehensive mission that touches peoples' lives here and now but also leads them to eternity. True mission is motivated by love, and not a feeling of obligation.

Our Saviour, the Lord Jesus, taught many things pertaining to our spiritual and practical lives. In every case however, He taught the truth about God and salvation.

God sent His son on a mission to die in place of human beings, who have disobeyed Him, and to reconcile them to Him. This mission is to make an offer of salvation known to all people and, thus, open the way for them to have redemption.

At its basic level, mission is letting the whole world know about Jesus and what He has done for each of us and what He promises to do for us now, and for eternity. In short, we who know about those promises have been called to tell others about them, as well.

Therefore, it sums up to the point that the gospel is all about Jesus. He addressed the whole being of His audience and invited them to make a decision in favour of God. Jesus audience "were amazed at His teaching, for He taught them as one having author-ity, and not as the teachers of the law" (Mark 1:22). Jesus authority gained credulity by the fact that He practised what He taught. Above all, He taught the truth because He is "the truth".

What's more is that Jesus presented His teachings to differ-ent audience, being careful to adapt His method to each person. Sometimes, His methods were flexible: A sermon at one time and a dialogue at another time. He could do His teaching in an open or in cameras as He deemed it possible.

In the end, Jesus showed the rewards of both the godly and ungodly. Now, through the gospel, His standard voice is calling us to follow Him, to renew our commitment to walk daily with Him by faith and in obedience.

Fragments, contains more about how you can earn salvation through the likeness of Jesus and His deep seated love for humanity. Thus, the Bible declares: "For God so loved the world..." (John 3:16).

Main Scriptural Text

"For God so loved the world that He gave His one and only Son, that whoever believes in Him shall not perish but have eternal life. For God did not send His Son into the world to condemn the world, but to save the world through Him. Whoever believes in Him is not condemned, but whoever does not believe stands condemned already because they have not believed in the name of God's one and only Son." (John 3:16–18)

1
God Is Eager to Save
(The Story of Jonah)

THE STORY OF Jonah, this rather unusual message of God, is one of the best known in the Bible. The prophet had been sent by God to warn Nineveh of impending destruction. He suspected that these non-Hebrew people might repent; Jonah knew that God's plan was to save Nineveh, not to destroy it. Perhaps that's why he, at first, tried to run away. Who's this Jonah, and why did he prove to be a recalcitrant and disobedient prophet of God?

Not much is known about Jonah or his family background. Second Kings 14:25 tells us that he lived in the northern part of Israel and ministered during the eighth century BC. The same text reveals that Jonah predicted a territorial expansion of Israel's kingdom.

Nineveh was historically one of the three great cities of Assyria, an important country situated by the Tigris River. Because God is the Lord of all nations and all peoples are accountable to Him (Amos 1–2), He sent His servant Jonah to warn the Ninevites of impending destruction. God's command recorded in Jonah 1:2 to "preach against it" can also be translated as "preach to it."

Assyrian cruelty was notorious. About a century later, the prophet Nahum called Nineveh a "bloody city...full of lies and robbery" (Nahum 3:1 NKJV). Jonah was sent to deliver God's message to such people. Perhaps it was the fear of the hated Assyrians, among other things, that prompted Jonah's attitude. When told by God to make a trip east to Nineveh, the prophet refused and tried to flee west by ship to Tarshish.

At first, all things appeared to work well for Jonah, but then the Lord God sent a great storm against the ship in order to teach His servant the lesson that no one can hide from God.

Jonah ran from God because he did not want to do God's will. Even now, people have many reasons to run away from God. Some do it because they do not know Him personally. Others reject even the idea of God and His Word. While people's motives vary, in many cases, they flee God in order not to feel guilty about the way in which they live. After all, if there is no higher power to answer to, why not do whatever you want? There are even some Christians who avoid God when He calls them to do something that they do not want to do, something that really goes against their inherently selfish and sinful nature.

In Jonah 1, God wants to halt Jonah's escape, so He stirs up such a severe storm that it threatens to wreck the ship. The seamen call on their gods for help. Due to the severity of the storm, they feel that someone must have provoked the anger of the gods. They cast lots to decide who will be the first to volunteer information about himself that might expose such an offense. For the casting of lots, each individual brings an identifiable stone or wooden marker. The markers are placed in a container that is shaken until one of the markers comes out. The lot falls on Jonah, who now confesses his sins and urges the seamen to throw him into the sea.

This story is remarkable because in it, the non-Hebrew seamen act positively, while Jonah the prophet is presented in a negative light. Although they worship many gods, the seamen show a great respect for the Lord Almighty God to whom they pray. They are also tender-hearted towards the Lord's servant Jonah, which is why they go out of their way to try to row back to land. Finally, they agree with Jonah that he should be thrown overboard. With this done, the storm stops, and the seamen sacrifice to God and praise Him.

Jonah's confession of faith in God as Creator of the sea and land underscores the futility of his attempts to escape from God's presence. The immediate cessation of the storm after the men throw Jonah into the sea shows them that God, as Creator, has control of the sea. Because of this, the seamen worship God all the more. How long their newfound fear and reverence for the Creator last? We are not told. There is no doubt, however, that they do learn something about Him from this experience.

When Jonah was thrown into the sea, a big fish swallowed him at God's bidding. Jonah must have thought that death indeed was going to be the only way to escape the mission to Nineveh. But the big fish (not called a whale in the book) was an instrument of salvation for the prophet. Unlike Jonah, this creature responded promptly and obediently to God's commands (Jonah 1:17, 2:10).

God's providence worked in an amazing way here. However, even though some people scoff at the story, Jesus testified to its veracity (Matthew 12:40) and even used it in reference to His own death and bodily resurrection.

Jonah's psalm celebrates God's deliverance of him from the perilous depths of the sea. It is the only poetic part of the book. In it Jonah recalls his prayer for help as he was sinking deep into the waters and facing certain death. Becoming fully aware of his salvation, he thanks God for it. The hymn indicates that Jonah is familiar with biblical psalms of praise and thanksgiving.

Jonah's vow likely consisted of a sacrifice of thanksgiving. He was grateful that, though he deserved to die, God had shown him extraordinary mercy. In spite of his disobedience, the prophet Jonah still considered himself loyal to God because he had not succumbed to idol worship. Whatever his many character flaws, he was now determined to try to be faithful to his calling.

After such a miraculous deliverance, Jonah obeyed immediately when he was commanded by God the second time to go preach in Nineveh. In his proclamation, Jonah (3:1–4) used language reminiscent of God's destruction of Sodom and Gomorrah (Genesis 19). But in the original Hebrew, the word for "overthrown" (Genesis 19:21, 29; Jonah 3:4) from Jonah's proclamation can also have the meaning "changed" or "turned around" or "transformed" (Exodus 7:17, 20; 1 Samuel 10:6). Jonah's preaching of the divine message was not in vain.

The greatest achievement of Jonah's prophetic career was the repentance of the city. After the seamen, the Ninevites were the second group of non-Hebrews in the book to turn to God, and all because of their interactions with God's flawed messenger, Jonah. The results were astounding. To humble themselves before God, the people of Nineveh wore sackcloth, put ashes on their heads, and fasted. All these were external signs of sorrow and repentance.

The remarkable picture of a strong Assyrian monarch humbling himself in ashes before God is a sharp rebuke to many of Israel's proud rulers and people, at least those who persistently rejected the prophetic calls to repentance. Because of the book of Jonah's emphasis on God's grace and forgiveness, the Jewish people read it every year at the climactic point of the Day of Atonement, which celebrates God's forgiveness for their sins.

Jonah 4 reveals some startling things about the prophet. He seems to prefer to die rather than to witness God's grace and forgiveness. Whereas before Jonah had rejoiced in his deliverance from death (Jonah 2:7–9), now that the people of Nineveh live, he prefers to die (Jonah 4:2–3).

In contrast to Jonah, God is pictured in the Bible as someone who takes "no pleasure in the death of the wicked" (Ezekiel 33:11 NKJV). Jonah and many of his compatriots rejoiced in God's special mercies to the people of Israel but wished only His wrath on their enemies. Such hardness of heart is rebuked sternly by the book's message.

God saved the sailors, the Ninevites, and His disobedient prophet. His compassion is open to everyone, reaches even the worst sinners, transcends borders, and goes beyond our human limits and understanding.

God loves everyone. Though God chose the Hebrew nation as an instrument for sending the promised seed to the world (Genesis 22:18), nevertheless, His compassion never fails, and it was mightily manifested for all the people of the earth through the death of His only begotten Son Jesus.

Let's rise to the occasion and make a difference by being kind and considerate towards others. To some people, human beings have a choice whether or not to show compassion towards their neighbours. That is not the same for the child of God—the Christian! Let God know that you're a truly compassionate person.

Coming back to the story of Jonah, we can infer of Jonah's pride, arrogance, stubbornness, disobedience, unfaithfulness, impatience, grumbling, and altogether his bad temper—this was Jonah, a prophet of God.

To conclude, when we call ourselves Christians, we must, at the same time do what is right notwithstanding the situation we find ourselves in—we must do the right thing at all times. Moreover, as humans, we are quick to judge, but we must always remember that we are not perfect, we all have flaws, and therefore if we have anything we can do to help our neighbours, we should do it with all joy, and the God of heaven will reward us.

2
God Loves the World
(John 3:16)

WHICH OF US can simply but boldly deny the fact that our omnip-
otent God's love is so wonderful? Indeed, our God's love cannot be
measured; it is limitless. Such a love cannot be compared. God's
supreme love is without parallel. It is what is described in Christianity
as agape love—a love manifested that doesn't need any form of reciprocity. Human beings' love is rather contrary and ephemeral to that
of the Supreme Beings.

Consider the depth of love God showed to Adam and Eve when
the couple ate the forbidden fruit in the Garden of Eden. The story
unfolds that when God entered the Garden, He realised the sin
committed by this family, and found that the couple was naked,
He clothed them. This, obviously, would not be tolerated by any
human being. But our God is tolerant—an attribute of deep-seated
love.

The golden rule is that God loves everyone irrespective of one's
behaviour, character, race, or family background. God abhors all forms
of discrimination. When the non-Hebrew Ninevites sinned against the
heavenly God, the latter devised a mechanism to save them. God did
so by sending His prophet to warn them of impending destruction.

Though Jonah ran away from God's will to save the people of Nineveh, God used another means to save them. Is it not the same procedure the Lord God adopted to rescue the sailors aboard the ship, who worshipped many false gods? As a result of this rescue, the seamen sacrificed to the Lord and praised Him as well. What a wonderful manifestation of love!

God is not only a Creator who divided a channel for the overflowing water, the One who made "a path for the thunderbolt to cause it to rain on a land where there is no one" (Job 38:25–26 NKJV). God distributes His providence equitably among humanity, and that's why "He makes His sun rise on the evil and on the good, and sends rain on the just and on the unjust" (Matthew 5:45 NKJV).

God's infinite love generated in Him the plan of redemption when humanity fell. The fall of humanity filled all heaven with sorrow. The Son of God, heaven's gracious commander, was touched with pity for the fallen race. His heart was moved with infinite compassion as the lost world rose up before Him.

God was to be manifested in Jesus "reconciling the world unto Himself" (2 Corinthians 5:19). The coming of Christ into humanity was the solution to reconcile humanity with God. Though never losing His divinity, Christ was also fully human, and in that humanity He knew what it was like to suffer and struggle just as all humans do. Today, Jesus is pleading with God so that all human beings are forgiven. The crucial thing for everyone is that we should cling to Jesus for our salvation.

There is no special prerequisite to go to Jesus, "He so loved the world and whoever believes in Him shall not perish but have eternal life" (John 3:16). Say to Jesus, "Please, come into my life and reign in me." Notwithstanding, Christ forces no one to come to Him. But Christ is willing that you open your heart to Him so that He can come in to save you.

He Gave His Only Begotten Son to You.

The plan of salvation, at its core, remains simple. Humanity, through sin, alienated itself from God. God, through Christ, was to come to heal that estrangement.

Sacred history from the days of Eden replays this theme, in one manifestation or another, over and over again. Humanity, through its sins and disobedience, severs itself from God. God, ever seeking, tries to bring humankind back under the shadow of His wings (John 17:8).

It is no different here, where the world, full of turbulence, has broken and continues to break the relationship with God. God has been faithful to His side of the bargain; the people are the ones who haven't kept up their end. Despite several appeals to humanity to listen to the voice of God, many are those who have proved to be recalcitrant.

As a plan of redemption has done before, God sent His only begotten Son Jesus to rescue humanity from their evil deeds. When Jesus was on earth, His life and death best exemplified this sad reality. Jesus did everything possible to reach those who, despite His overtures, rejected Him. Notwithstanding this rejection by humanity, God would not relent on His efforts to speak with humanity. Who is Jesus?

Any rational being anywhere on the globe needs to declare his or her ignorance of Jesus. Perhaps one may say to oneself that one doesn't need the services of the Lord Jesus Christ in one's life. Such people obviously seem to be morbid, and they need to be rescued. The psalmist once said, "Rescue the perishing." Possibly, a worldwide crusade, in the form of mega prayer session, is crucial to help those people be aware that Jesus is the Creator of the universe.

Honestly speaking, so many people today think that they are self-sufficient in all their endeavours. They are satisfied with what they have and think that they do not need Jesus to come into their hearts and lives. A greater number of people globally have this to say: "We're satisfied with our treasures." Talk of money, estates, good medical facilities, mansions, and what have you. To some of these people, they claim the universality of power and prestige and abundance of legacies. "Jesus, for what?" they declare!

Just calm down and think that, no matter your status, one day your soul will need the spiritual services of the Saviour Jesus Christ. Read Mark 8:36 to alert yourself.

Jesus is divine, the Creator of the universe, including humankind. Humanity sinned. Adam's transgression brought wretchedness and death unto humanity. Who was to rescue man from this terrible state? Jesus, being the answer, was to sacrifice his life to bring life and immortality to the fallen state of humankind. At his creation, Adam, the first man on earth, was placed in dominion over the earth. But yielding to temptation, he was brought under the power of Satan. "A man is a slave to whatever has mastered him" (2 Peter 2:19). When humans became Satan's captives, the dominion that they held passed to their conqueror. Thus, Satan became "the god of this world" (See 2 Corinthians 4:4). Satan had usurped that power that was originally bestowed to humankind by God. But Jesus, by His sacrifice, paid the penalty of sin, thereby redeeming humanity from sin. Also, the sacrifice of Jesus helped humans recover their dominion, which Satan had fortified. All that was lost by the first Adam will be restored by the second Adam.

To achieve this, Jesus (the second Adam) had to be in human flesh to fulfil God's plan of salvation. Scripture presents Jesus as a true human being. He was born as a baby and grew up as a child, increasing in wisdom and in stature. The grace of God was upon Him (Luke 2:40, 52), and he had brothers and sisters (Matthew 13:55–56). He ate (Matthew 9:10–11). He slept (Luke 8:23). He was tired and thirsty (John 4:6–7). He was sorrowful and troubled (Matthew 26:37–38). We should remember the emotional reaction our world evoked in Jesus: "Jesus wept" (John 11:35).

To the casual observer, Jesus of Nazareth seemed to be a common man who walked among people as one of the multitude. Many of His contemporaries did not recognise in Him anything more than a man (John 7:46). People treated Him as one of them (Matthew 11:19); they laughed at Him (Luke 8:53); mocked and beat Him (Luke 22:63). To them, Jesus was just another human being.

Unfortunately, they failed to perceive that there is more to be found in this title. According to Daniel 7:13–14, "One like the Son of Man, coming with the clouds of heaven! He came to the Ancient of Days, and received everlasting dominion, glory and a kingdom" (NKJV). The Jews identified this Son of humankind with the Messiah. So when Jesus used this title, He was revealing, in a half-concealed way, that He was also the promised, the incarnate Christ.

In addition to the above human qualities exhibited by Christ, the Hebrews expressed some incredible truth about our Lord Jesus Christ. They say, "For we do not have a high priest who is unable to empathise with our weaknesses, but we have one who has been tempted in every way, just as we are—yet he did not sin"(Hebrews 4:15). That is the feeling of our infirmities, and as we all know, the feelings of our infirmities can be pretty bad.

Jesus responded to all questions in an emotional state while on His earthly ministry. Today, human beings are all damaged goods and are getting worse every day. Sin has taken its toll on our emotional health. So often, instead of us being in control of our emotions, they control us, even to the point of pushing us into radically wrong choices that cause us even more grief and sorrow. Fortunately, that doesn't always need to be the case. Jesus had something better for us, and that was why God sent Him to bring all human problems under His loving sovereignty. Finally, when He took our sins on the cross, He nailed all our burdens and problems on the cross so that after believing in Him, we no longer struggle with sin.

Emotions are vital part of the human personality. They can be powerful motivators, both for good and for evil. Depending on the type of emotions, they can make us happy, sad, fearful, or joyous. Positive emotions can bring a feeling of satisfaction and well-being; negative ones tend to cause pain and anguish. God wants all His children to enjoy the effects of positive emotions. However, because of sin and bad choices, we often face the adverse effects of negative emotional experiences.

Ammon's "love" for Tamar, for example, could not have been true love but rather a strong sexual drive, because as soon as he achieved his goal, he "hated" her intensely (2 Samuel 13:15). Tamar must have felt humiliated—a very bad emotion indeed. When Absalom heard this episode, he planned to kill Ammon in order to avenge his sister's rape—a wicked act.

Positive emotions, however, promote good health, longevity, and happiness. The end product of positive emotions is that the more positive your outlook and emotions, the better overall health you can enjoy, and the more others want to get closer to you. Galatians 5:22 elucidates this fact.

Perhaps the most outstanding emotion one needs to exercise is love. Though love is more than emotion; it is the supreme emotion. God is love, and it is His plan for His children to experience love for others and from others. This is because love brings about an array of other positive feelings and emotions that can be translated into highly desirable behaviours.

We learn from the Bible that Jesus's emotional manifestation was characterised by compassion. Lepers often were treated with disdain in those days, and even in our days. Because Jesus felt compassion for a leper, He cured him instantly. Consider also people who lacked basic physical necessities and those who were without leadership or directions or alms; Jesus was so quick to come to their aid.

In Mark 9:36, Jesus held little children and showed love and affection for them. He also touched diseased people in order to communicate divine healing power. In the encounter with the rich young ruler (Mark 10:21–22), Jesus loved him even though the young man did not follow the master's direction. In an instant, both experienced strong emotions.

Apart from Jesus's emotional manifestations, He taught a lot of things. Prostitution and adultery are traditional paths into sexual immorality and addiction (Proverbs 5:3–14). In addition, other forms of sex addiction are available today, such as pornography, cybersex, and exploitative sex. Pornography is causing a staggering problem in the society. Sex immorality has plagued a lot of people in recent times, even though those people who are involved claim it as a lucrative job. God is willing to grant full pardon and freedom to anyone trapped in sex addiction. Submission to Him is crucial (James 4:7).

Jesus taught humanity how to manage guilt and stress, how to reinforce relationships among people, and how to achieve good thinking and self-esteem, among other things. Perhaps the subject of jealousy needs further explanation. Some biblical personalities who allowed jealousy to impact their behaviour were Lucifer (Isaiah 14:12–17), Cain (Genesis 4), Joseph's brothers (Genesis 37:18–36), King Saul (1 Samuel 18–27), Haman (Esther 3:4–5), and the chief priests of the New Testament (Mark 15:10; John 11:47). The result was always disastrous. How fascinating, too, that all of these individuals enjoyed high status and privileges. Yet all fell into the trap of hating someone else for what they were not or what they had. The life of Joseph, for example, has been compared to the life of Jesus. Jealousy moved his brothers to sell him as a slave; some chief priests and elders were jealous of Jesus, and that jealousy fuelled their actions against Him. While Joseph was sold, Jesus was falsely accused. The evil actions against Joseph ultimately led to good; the same thing happened with Jesus, in that the evil done against Him was turned to good as well.

God warns us away from such erroneous path and urges His children to love their neighbours to the point of rejoicing with them in their gifts, achievements, and possessions as if they were our own.

When sin ruined everything—when anger, jealousy, greed, hatred, and violence contaminated the world, the natural environment also became intolerable. The Flood, however, changed the portrait of the earth. Now goodness and beauty remain in the natural world. Nature also can provide joy, happiness, and well-being to compensate partially for the misery caused by sin. Since nature can be a source of mental and physical health, it is up to humanity to draw ever closer to the Creator. It must be emphasised at this juncture that time is an element of nature. In communion with God, one needs a quiet time with Him. Such quiet time with the Maker can bring healing and peace to our bodies and souls. Note that God's gifts come through nature. Therefore, it is erroneous to say that you don't need Jesus in your life. Your survival on earth depends largely on your Creator—Master Jesus. If you have ignored Him, start reprogramming your mind with God's word. Every human being needs Jesus.

> "His divine power has given us everything we need for life and godliness through our knowledge of Him who called us by His own glory and goodness. Through these He has given us His very great and precious promises, so that through them you may participate in the divine nature and escape the corruption in the world caused by evil de-sires." (2 Peter 1:3–4)

We need Jesus. Today, on the news, you hear "Man killed wife over diner delay" or "Wife killed husband out of jealousy" or "Child killed parents for rituals." This is the world we live in. Can someone rescue us from the sinfulness of this world? Absolutely not! Why don't we go to the One Who created the earth as the dwelling place for humanity for our rescue?

Bear in mind that some Supreme Being brought you into exis-tence. Consequently, you need to adore, adhere to, and respect Him. If you decide to neglect Christ you are doomed forever. In order not to perish, listen to Jesus. He was brought into the world for the salva-tion of the wretched sinner like you. God loves you.

3
The Father's Love
(The Story of the Prodigal Son)

JESUS'S MISSION ON earth was: "To seek and to save the lost." (Matthew Luke 19:10). What then was lost? Needless to say, it was humanity itself that chose to alienate itself from his Maker (God), chose to die, and is now filled with fear and disappointment and despair. If nothing were done on our behalf, all would perish and be lost. For this reason, there should be a rescuer for the perishing. Thanks be to Jesus for coming to our rescue. Jesus the Saviour serves as a bridge, an intermediary and a link between humanity and God.

God's purpose in creating humans was to have fellowship with them. God and humanity were for one another. God is our Father (Matthew 6:9), and we are His children (John 1:12). Second, God created humankind in His own image so that humans could reflect the character and personality of God. Psalm 82:6 declares: "You are gods, and all of you are children of the Most High God" (NKJV). Third, to share God's rule. God said: "Let us make man in our image, according to our likeness; and let them have dominion..." (Genesis 1:26 NKJV). Human beings were created to share God's authority. In simplicity, human beings were created to reign with God in one kingdom, and that kingdom is the Kingdom of God.

The Bible is a story of God seeking after lost humanity. From Genesis to Revelation are the truths of God's willingness to save humanity from getting lost. The central theme of the Bible is love. Luke the writer illustrates this truth by using three important parables: The lost sheep (Luke 15:4–7), the lost coin (verses 8–10), and the lost son (verses 11–32). Who is Luke?

Luke is a Gentile doctor, a convert of course whose letter is referred to as "The Gospel according to Luke." He also writes the Book of Acts, which is also referred to as "The Acts of the Apostles." Having travelled with Apostle Paul, Luke was able to write all that he saw while trekking with him. Under the inspiration of the Holy Spirit, Luke wrote a two-volume work, "The Origin and History of the Christian Church." The Gospel according to Luke is the longest in the New Testament. For a better biographical sketch of Jesus, why not consult the Gospel according to Saint Luke?

As said earlier, Dr. Luke's illustrations on the loss of humanity are explained in three parables: The lost sheep, the lost coin, and the lost son. For the purpose of our discussion, our focus is restricted to the last one, the lost son. This parable could also be called the parable of the lost son, the parable of the prodigal son, or the return of the lost son. The Bible makes us understand that it is a loving story of the Father.

Known in history as the most beautiful story ever told on the forgiving nature of love, the parable of the prodigal son (Luke 15:11–32), narrated only by Luke, may well be called the parable of the loving father and two lost sons. One son chose the lawlessness of the distant land over the love of the father. The other son chose to stay at home but did not fully know the love of the father. The younger son symbolises the lost, basically tax collectors and the sinners of the day (Luke 15:2), and the elder brother represents the self-righteous (the Pharisees and teachers of the law of that day, Luke 15:2). The major theme of this parable seems not to be so much the conversion of the sinner but rather the restoration of a believer into fellowship with the Father. In the story of the prodigal son, we witness the father waiting and watching eagerly for his son's return. This story demonstrates God's love for each individual sinner and His attentiveness towards all humanity. In addition, the story is seen as the graciousness of the father overshadowing the sinfulness of the son, as it is the memory of the father's goodness that brings the prodigal son to repentance (Romans 2:4).

In this story, there are three stages:

- The rejection of home—away from home
- The return to home—coming back home
- The reception at home—received at home

In ordinary parlance, the word "prodigal" means carelessly and foolishly spending money or wasting precious time. The *Cambridge English Dictionary* defines "prodigal" as a male, whether a man or a boy, who has left his loving family in order to do something that the family does not sanction, and has now returned home, feeling sorry for what he has done. This behaviour could also be associated with a female.

The meaning of the story is unfolded when we turn to verse 12 of Luke 15. The younger son asks his father for his fair share of the estate, which would have been half of what his older brother would receive. This younger son's decision to demand of his father his portion of the property was an impulsive urge. The younger son gave a command to the father: "Give me" (Luke 15:12). What an impulsion! The younger son had no right to ask of his father the share of his estates while the father was still alive. Sin often causes one to behave that way. Instead of rebuking his son, the father patiently grants him his request. The younger son might have heard friends or neighbours discussing the glitter and glamour of distant lands. Perhaps life at home was too rigid and sometimes boring. The distant land offered him life without restrictions. The father was too protective; his love was too embracing. But the son wanted freedom. And in view of this, the son sought to rebellious act "Give me."

Life is full of choices. Often, you hear that God is a dictator and Christianity is a means of manipulating or controlling people. The truth is that God does not force anyone to accept His word; neither does He make strict rules for us—we make our plans, according to Proverbs 16:19. God said to the Israelites, "See, I set before you today life and prosperity, death and destruction" (Deuteronomy 30:15). Jesus said to His disciples, "Follow Me." (Matthew 4:19, 8:22). Here, you can choose to follow Jesus or not (Matthew 9:9; Mark 10:17–22). The choice is yours! And that was what the younger son did. He chose to leave his father's home and go to a far country.

No sooner had the father shared his estates between the two sons than the younger son cashed in his entire share and set off to the "far country." The far country was a place far away from the father's home. It was a land full of "riotous living" (verse 13). In the New Testament epistles, riotous living symbolises drunkenness (See Ephesians 5:18), rebelliousness (See Titus 1:6), and debauchery that includes "lewdness, lust, drunkenness, revelries, drinking, wild parties and abominable idolatries" (See 1 Peter 4:3–4).

The "far country" could also mean being alienated from God. Or the "far country" in our world today could be compared to your porn sites, or worldly friends who lead you to sin, or your old carnal nature that you are not able to mortify.

In the story of the prodigal son, such pleasures of godless living wasted away his health and wealth, and soon he became moneyless, friendless, and foodless. His glittering life ended up in a gutter. His life became so wretched, and he did not know what to do. There arose a mighty famine. He starved to the point of being in a perpetual want. He found employment in caring for pigs. This is described as a high fate for a Jew. It is an abomination for Jews to deal with issues of pigs. And this young man had found himself in this job to the extent that he would even eat the food of the pigs—slop. What an abomination! What a shame!

When his employer realised that this young man was feeding on the food of the hogs, the boss gave him a word of caution, telling him that if he were caught eating the food of the animals, he would be sacked. Being depressed in life, the young man recalled the occasions when even his father's labourers were eating decent food. He was now starving. His decision now was to return home—his forsaken home. His painful experience now helped him acknowledge the fact that going back home would offer him relief and hope (See Psalms 147:11). From here, it is clear that, apart from God, there is no hope. This prodigal son was willing to give up his rights as his father's son and take on the position of his servant.

So when the prodigal son came back to his senses, he went back home with a piece of note in his hand to plead with the father, "Make me" (Luke 15:17–19). This means that the father should make him (the son) whatever he (the father) pleases. It is clear that this speech is a demonstration of true humility and repentance, not based on compulsion; it is from within a sinner's mind. The son realised he had no right to claim a blessing upon his return to his father's household, nor did he have anything to offer, except a life of service, in repentance of his previous actions. This son was seriously seeking for hope, forgiveness, peace, and mercy. And this is all about the doctrine of conversion. One pastor has this to say: "Ending a life of slavery to sin through conversion to the Father and faith in Christ Jesus and becoming a slave to righteousness, offering one's body as a living sacrifice" (Romans 6:6–18).

The journey home was at last ended (Luke 15:17–20). It was a journey full of genuine repentance and contrition of heart. Before the son's arrival, the father was praying a long time and waiting for his son, perhaps daily searching the distant road, hoping for his son coming; he ran to greet his son (verse 20). Is it normal for a father to break the convention for this wayward child who had sinned against him? The obvious answer is that he *loved* him and was eager to show him that love can possibly restore the relationship. When the father saw his son, not only did he throw his arms around him, but he also greeted him with a kiss of love (See 1 Peter 5:14).

The prodigal son returns to the father with a contrite heart – a changed heart. First, there is an acknowledgment of the father as "my father" (verse 18). The son now needs to lean on trust, his father's love and forgiveness, just as we must lean on and trust in our heavenly Father's love and forgiveness. When we ask God's forgiveness, no matter the magnitude of our sins, He will forgive us. Why then do you delay asking for God's forgiveness?

The second point is confession. In the third point, there was a clear manifestation of contrition; hence he declares, "I am no longer worthy" (verse 19). The last point at this stage is a petition offered to the father: "Make me" (verse 19). As the father was waiting and saw the son "a great way off," he had compassion and ran, and he fell on his son's neck and kissed him. This is indeed the true character of God; a forgiving Father. Do you possess such a character? If you don't, then pray for a manifestation of such character to be part of you.

The father embraced the son, clothed him with a new robe, put an expensive ring on his finger and a pair of shoes on his feet, and ordered a grand feast in his honour. The entire family were all in grand jubilation. If leaving the home was death, the return was a resurrection, and worthy of rejoicing. All these things represent what we receive in Christ upon salvation. Instead of condemnation, there is rejoicing for the son who had been dead but now is alive, who once was lost but now is found (verse 24). Are you like that? If yes, come to Christ for resurrection and salvation. You are lost, and the Father is eagerly waiting for your return. Will you run to Him?

Note that a fattened calf is used to prepare the feast, and blood was shed, signifying atonement for sins (Hebrews 9:22).

The return of the prodigal son did not attract the attention of the older son. The older son failed in "acknowledging that the prodigal son is his own brother" (verse 30). The elder son's attitude towards the father is the same as that of the Pharisees who accused Jesus: "This man welcomes sinners and eats with them" (Luke 15:2). The father's final word with his elder son reflects heaven's attitude to all repentant sinners: "It was right that we make merry and be glad, for your brother was dead and is now alive, and was lost and is found" (verse 32).

This older brother's focus was on himself, and as a result, there was no joy in his brother's arrival. He was so consumed with issues of equity and justice that he failed to see the value of his brother's genuine repentance and return. This elder son failed to recognise that whoever loves his brother lives in the light, and there is nothing in him to make him stumble. But whoever hates his brother is in darkness; he does not know where he is going, because the darkness has blinded him (1 John 2:9–11). Possibly, this son saw his brother's return as a threat to his own inheritance. Soon, he entreated his father for receiving his younger brother. Following the story carefully, it is crystal clear that the elder brother wanted his brother to receive the consequences of his wayward life. But the father's love was immeasurable.

The picture represented in this episode is that we should all respond to repentant sinners as well (James 5:19–20). This is because "all have sinned and fall short of the glory of God" (Romans 3:23). Everybody is included in that "all," and that's why Isaiah is saying, "All of us have become like one who is unclean, and all our righteous acts are like filthy rags" (Isaiah 64:6a).

"Where sin increased, grace increased all the more" (Romans 5:20), and through this grace we find ourselves saved. Therefore, don't be boastful of yourself in any endeavour of life. If you want to pride yourself, you must do it in Christ (See 1 Corinthians 1:31); thank God for saving your life.

Ostensibly, countless multitudes are on their way to Christ for salvation. Among these are armed robbers, prostitutes, drug-addicts, rapists, murderers, adulterers, fornicators, backsliders, and all those who cause extensive pain to their neighbours. What should be our reaction while these people are coming to Christ? Are we going to judge them so that they go back to their sinful ways? That should not be our lifestyle! We should rather accept them for who they are. In Christ, all manner of judgement ceases. Jesus says, "Do not judge, or you too will be judged." (Matthew 7:1). As Christians, we are not permitted to remind any sinner of his or her past life, but rather to encourage them to do their best for Christ.

Life Application from the Story.
In this parable, the two sons born to the same father represent two character traits. The older one demonstrates loyalty, perseverance, and industry. The younger one, however, is reluctant to work, unwilling to be accountable, and unprepared to assume responsibility. It seems one son is faithful, hardworking, and respectful, while the other is unfaithful, lazy, and disrespectful. Nobody understands why two sons born to the same father behave differently.

Luke 15:12 unfolds an information-seeking dialogue between the younger son and the father, the former's determination to ask his father for his fair share of his estates. This son is given the choice to go. All through the Bible, we can see this same principle. God allows human beings the freedom to make their own choices, to go their own way, and to live as they want. God forces no one to be obedient to Him. If He did at all, He would have forced Adam and Eve to be obedient in the Garden of Eden. Likewise, the father does not force his son to stay home. Of course, as we know so well, our choices come with consequences that we don't always imagine or foresee.

The young, adventurous, and energetic man goes to a world full of fun for enjoyment. Perhaps life in the family might appear dull and boring to him. So moving far away from the family may, to him, solve such boredom he was experiencing at home.

This son eventually finds himself in a distant land full of anarchy and "of riotous living." Rebellion, drunkenness, and wild parties are the order of the day. Such pleasures of godless living waste away his health and wealth, and soon he becomes moneyless, friendless, and foodless. Just picture yourself in this terrible situation. What a destitute condition! The only thing that the son ought to do is to come back to ask for pardon from his father and possibly say, "Father, I am really sorry. Please forgive me."

After all, who among us, at times, hasn't been really sorry not so much for our sins and mistakes but for the consequences of them, especially when we get caught? In the process, if the young man practised fornication and picked up gonorrhoea, AIDS, or any sexually transmitted diseases, wouldn't you have pity for him?

This parable is applicable to young people of our modern era. They usually rush in life, and many of them end up in foreign countries. Of course, all of these young people have their reasons for this unwholesome exodus. If their lives in those faraway areas are godless, they end up in fertile grounds for so many social vices. Why? This is because they run away from being checked by their parents. They are without constant Christian teachings and leadership.

Sometimes in life, we need the bad consequences of our actions to awaken us to the reality of our sins. That is, only after suffering comes from our actions do we truly repent of those actions and not just regret the actions.

The prodigal son gave in to his lust for pleasure and jumped headlong into a life of full-blown sin, squandering his entire inheritance on fast living, booze, and prostitutes. Now, he is reaping the consequences. The consequences of the son's sins are many. His sins cost him not only his financial stability and comfortable home but his dignity, self-respect, reputation, purity, and good conscience. "A man reaps what he sows" (Galatians 6:7–8).

Thousands of students, especially those in high school or college, possess the same nature as the prodigal son. When they think that their homes appear to be an "inferno" simply because their parents often put up the mechanisms of checks and balance to educate them, naturally they flee their homes to enter into sinful ventures—fornication, boozing, gambling, occultism, you name them. The consequences of these actions are not only dangerous but catastrophic. Consequently, some of the females end up in premarital sex, teenage pregnancy, and illegal abortion. What's more is that most of these young people lose their purity, reputation, and self-respect. Their bodies are defiled such that the temple of God is destroyed.

God loves such people, and that's why it is said that we should "flee from sexual immorality...Or don't you know that your bodies are temples of the Holy Spirit, who is in you, whom you have received from God, and you are not your own?" (1 Corinthians 3:16–17; 6:18–19). God, through Apostle Paul, admonishes humanity to refrain from those acts, "for you were bought at a price, therefore glorify God in your body and in your spirit, which are God's" (1 Corinthians 6:20 NKJV). If you are in this state, Jesus says, "Come to me, all you who are weary and burdened, and I will give you rest" (Matthew 11:28). Jesus is patiently waiting to rescue you from this sinful world. Jesus portrays the father as waiting for his son, perhaps daily searching the distant road, hoping for his appearance. The father's compassion assumes some knowledge of the son's pitiful state, as soon as the son returns. The father is filled with joy and doesn't want even his son's confession. Likewise, when we decide to repent of our sins and return to Christ, the Bible says, "There is rejoicing in the presence of the angels of God over one sinner who repents" (Luke 15:10).

We should notice that when the son ran into trouble in the faroff country, he sought help from "a citizen of that country" instead of seeking help from his father. The citizen did not love him. Rather, the citizen exploited him as cheap labour during an economic downturn, offering him demeaning manual labour in a piggery. If you sin against God, and you are reaping the consequences of it, simply come back to God. He is ever ready to forgive you. God would not make you wretched, nor would He make you suffer as the prodigal suffered even among his own friends in a distant area.

Before his journey back home, the son was prompted internally. The Bible emphatically says, "When he came back to his senses," he admitted to himself that he had made a foolish mistake, committed a sin against heaven (God) and his father. Just like any attitudes and self-concepts change as we journey towards God, the prodigal son changed his attitudes when he was about to get home. Look at the order: The father ran to meet his son, fell on him, and kissed him. The father also told his servants to bring "the best robe" and placed it on his son. The father didn't wait for the son to enter the house and have a bath before placing the best robe of Christ's righteousness on him, and neither did he asks the son, "What do you have to say?" or say, "Have you seen the consequences of your foolish act?" No! All that was needed was provided for the son right there and then.

What is so amazing here, too, is that there is no "I told you so!" from the father. When dealing with people who come back after falling away from you or the family, do not make such a statement. As parents, when your children come back to their senses, you should accept them. If you are wife whose husband has left you, and later, he decides to come back to you, accept him for restoration. Especially teenagers, who lack self-control should know that there is something wrong with them. "A man without self-control is like a city broken into and left without walls." (Proverbs 25:28 ESV). This means that anyone can come into the city and besiege it and take away everything that belongs to the people. When you are unable to control yourself, you are driven by any worldly passion that comes your way, and if it is smoking, you easily give in because you are unable to say no to it. Likewise, if it is stealing, you easily give in. Be careful! Go before the Lord in prayer and you will surely find solace there. Naturally, the Father would put on you "the best robe" to restore you.

Our turbulent world is full of people in the grip of sins very difficult to stop. Countless multitudes are still lost in sin. Husbands are not exempted. Apart from the legally married wife, they also have other girlfriends and concubines to their advantage. Just realise that you have sinned against the Father. Confess to Him, and "the best robe" will be put on you. Wives who are not submissive to their husband should also know that they are disrespectful to God and their husbands. Change by cultivating the fruit of the Spirit (See Galatians 5:22–23). No matter how wretched you find yourself, just pray for God's touch. The Father's restoration will bring overwhelming joy and unfathomable happiness to the sinner as well as the courts of heaven above.

From the story of the prodigal son, we gather that the father wants, right away, to cover the shame of the son's mistakes. It is a message for all of us to forget those who hurt us and focus on the present. Let's forget the past and start a new life. When Christ forgives the sinner, He does not remember the sins anymore. We are advised to do likewise—forgiving the sins of others. Remember that some of the worst sins are not known now, but one day will be. Apostle Paul is telling us that we need to forget the past and press toward the mark of the high calling or the future inheritance (Philippians 3:13–14).

Also, the father's actions in this story are a beautiful picture of how God welcomes us back into the fold. God does not wait for us to come all the way. Rather, He comes to meet us as we are and where we are. God does not put anyone on probation; He restores us instantly to our place as His dear children. (See John 1:12–13).

The story shows how most of us would react if this happened to us. I think the majority us would be upset if our younger brothers and sisters ran away for a long time and did a whole bunch of bad things and then came home, and our parents threw a big party for them?

The amazing side of the story is that the father, who had been wronged, was forgiving. But the eldest son, who had not been wronged, was unforgiving. In this parable, Jesus gives a clear picture of God and what God is like. God is truly kinder than us. God is a loving Father, and His love is incomparable.

Tit-for-tat, they say, is fair play. But the Bible makes us understand that "tit-for-tat" is a sin. The Gospel according to Matthew admonishes us that we should avoid tit-for-tat and live generously with others. Again, Christ advised His disciples to break the old written laws, "Love your friend" and "Hate your enemy," and love their enemies. He also said to them: "When someone gives you a hard time, respond with the energies of prayer, for then you are working out your true selves, your God-created selves. This is what God does" (Matthew 5:42–48).

Sometimes in life, you could hurt someone and some would also hurt you. But when we are hurt, we begin to break away from all those who have caused us pains. Gradually, we begin to isolate ourselves from everyone, and we actually inflict more pain on ourselves than the original hurt. Hate no one, no matter how much they've wronged you. Someone said: "Forgiveness is what we all want to receive from others but when someone offends us we hesitate to forgive them." I quote some excellent remarks on forgiveness and peacefulness from Martin Luther King Jr. and Mahatma Gandhi:

"Forgiveness is not an occasional act, but it is
a constant attitude."

—Martin Luther King Jr.

"Whenever you are confronted with an opponent,
conquer him with love."

—Mahatma Gandhi

As Christians, we imitate Christ's manner of life. This is seen in the example of Paul. Apostle Paul said to the Corinthians to imitate him just as he imitates Christ (1 Corinthians 4:16, 11:1). A preacher once said: "We cannot die for the sins of others. But following Christ's manner of suffering unjustly for doing right, we return love for hate." We are daily prompted by our instincts to do the right thing. Follow your instincts when you are prompted by the Holy Spirit to do the right thing.

Serving Christ involves the heart and mind. Serving God with all your mind means that it is only God who controls your mind. Worship the Lord with all your heart means that God is at the zenith of your affairs. However, while God lives in you, Satan tries to adulterate the mind but the Holy Spirit is there as a rescuer. The moment you despise God, you are easily going to perish. Denounce sin because a sinful person has no place in God's kingdom. Allow Jesus to rule your life.

Factors That Influence Teenagers to Social Vices.

Who is to blame for children's waywardness? Watching the current trend of what is happening in our world, I've observed that most parents are authors of their children's waywardness. Opinion polls suggest that most parents have abandoned the training and nurturing of their children because these parents, instead of using their precious time for the formation of their wards, rather turn their attention to their businesses. At this stage, let us consider some of the causes that lead most young people into social vices. The following are some of the causes:

- Lack of role models at home
- Provocative parents
- Constant inter-parental conflict
- Conflicts between step-parents and step-children
- Conflicts among siblings
- Lack of encouragement from parents
- Lack of comfort affection from parents
- Lack of warning from parents

Lack of role models at home can be a big problem for children in the family. Consider for a moment what children will say when parents behave contrary to what they say or do at home. When this happens, few children are able to listen to their parents. Notwithstanding, God expects children to obey their parents. Parents are therefore advised to be faithful in all things because their children are learning and copying them.

Provocative parents. The truth is that no one chooses to have his or her own parents. God gives children parents who would love them and care for their needs. No matter how illiterate your parents are, they are still important in your life. Likewise, parents should be thankful but cherish these gifts. (See Psalms 127:3). In this case, we are referring to the children they have from God (See James 1:17). Again, the Bible warns parents not to exasperate their children to anger but rather they are to bring them up in the fear of God (Ephesians 6:4).

One issue that drives most children away from the comfort of their home is the provocative act of parents. In a family where children cannot make basic decisions for themselves, pose a threat to their upbringing. Children under a calibre of this atmosphere take advantage of any opportunity that comes on their way to experiment what they've never had chance to do, whether good or bad. It is therefore necessary for parents to reason with their children and not being too harsh on them. Most parents make mistakes all the time. At times, they blame children for their own mistakes. One of the hardest things for parents to learn is how to talk to their children. It is easy to say things that hurt your children and you may not realise. Please, be careful how you speak to your children.

Constant inter-parental conflict. There is no family without conflict. Conflict is part of family life. Persistent conflicts, provocations and arguments within married couples are incontestable. But when parents continuously fight, argue, and call each other names like "Fat" "Slut" "Fool" "Bitch", these profanities do not educate children about the decency of marriage. "Exposure to verbal and physical aggression between marriage couple may hurt your children's ability to identify and control emotions," according to a longitudinal study led by the Steinhardt School of Culture, Education, and Human Development.

Conflicts between step-parents and step-children. Living with step-parents or step-children is difficult. Studies tell us that half of all marriages end up in divorce, and new step-families are formed every year. Thus, many families have challenges adjusting to the new living environment. Some say, your home is where your heart is. But this is not the same for most step-parents and step-children living in the same home. Some step-mothers say that "I am married to their father, and not the children." Step-children also tend to say that "After all, he or she is not my biological father or biological mother; I can do whatever I choose to do." What parents should do is that, there should be family meetings whenever new step-families are formed. To make this a reality, each one's challenges must be made known, and thereafter, every member of the family must work on how to bring joy into the family and help one another.

Conflicts among siblings. Living together as a family can be complex, especially when children become teenagers. The family is the immediate agent to settle conflicts. Whenever there is conflict, parents must allow all siblings to express their feeling during a family meeting to help alleviate harboured feelings. Once parents have listened to each party, instead of continuing a blame game syndrome, they need to address issues genuinely so that each party will willingly or genuinely say sorry and ask for forgiveness. This will help the family to stay together in love, unity, peace and harmony.

Lack of encouragement from parents could make your children wayward. Children need encouragement from their parents. But the sad news is that most children never listen to encouraging words from their parents. Let us listen to how some parents talk with their children. "Are you deaf?" "You are 24 years old and still unmarried; go out there and see many of your age mates who are now married and living on their own. Ama...leave my house!" Sooner or later, your children become broken in heart and begin to isolate themselves from you.

Whenever there is lack of encouragement and motivation, children turn to people who see the best in them and listen to their advice. But the sad news is that these people may have bad influence in your neighbourhood. They may be drunkards, rebels, drug-addicts, disrespectful, and what have you, who may be influencing and leading your children into paths that deviate in the end from the righteousness of God.

Parents must be careful and duly sensitive in the upbringing of their children. Let your children know how precious they are—to you! Have fun with them. Let your children be your wealth. Invest more in your children's life. An old woman used to tell her children, "Your children are your wealth." Are your children your wealth?

Lack of comfort affection from parents. Children need comfort and sometimes petting from their parents. There are times children become discouraged, hurt, confused, or sad. During this period, children need comforting. How well do you comfort your children when facing such difficulties?

To be a good comforter to your children, you have to be accessible to them. Children are comforted when they know their parents are available and make them happy whenever they run to them in times of need.

Lack of warning from parents. Parents should warn their children from taking wrong decisions. Nonetheless, parents should reason with their children. But the missing link is that, many parents confuse warning with threats. "I will kill you when you steal." "I swear it will not end well with you." – These are some of their threats. Actually, this behaviour of most parents makes their children live in fear and interpret warnings as threats. Using the Bible as a moral compass will help especially Christian parents in training their children. Know that whenever warnings become full of provocations and threats, children become threatened.

To conclude, do you find yourself in the situation of the prodigal son? What sin are you carrying such that it has created a gulf between you and your Father (God)? When do you want to come to your senses to go to your Maker (God)? Strength and grace have been provided through Christ. He is waiting to strip your strained and polluted garment with sin and give you a "new garment." Why delay?

4

The Golden Rule
(Love Your Neighbour as Yourself)

"GOLDEN," A TWO-SYLLABLE word, is an English adjective qualifying the noun "Rule." Anything described as Golden is of paramount importance. Such an object is worthy in degree and importance. It is not fake but possesses the qualities of being invaluable, priceless, pure, excellent, and even splendid. Taking the noun phrase "Golden Rule" in its totality could simply mean "guiding principles," a moral principle used to refer to human conduct. It could, therefore, be inferred from this, that the Golden Rule has some relationship with human life. The Golden Rule could not be more applicable to the lives of human beings.

The Golden Rule that should connect the lives of humanity is thus: "One should treat others as one would like others to treat oneself." This universal declaration can be said as "the act of putting others first." The biblical context as declared by Master Jesus is "Do to others what you would have them do to you" (Matthew 7:12; Luke 6:31). The beginning of the statement is in the imperative form. Jesus said "Do," meaning we are commanded to perform an act on His behalf. This is an instruction Jesus gave while delivering His Sermon on the Mount of Olives (Matthew 5:1–11). Earlier, Jesus had healed a great multitude and preached the gospel of the Kingdom of God to those people.

It is always the intention of God to give His people guidance through the Bible, the Holy Spirit, and Jesus, as well as the prophets, on how to treat one another. However, our selfish nature bars us from treating our neighbours just as ours. Irrespective of this propensity, God intends His children to be kind and considerate to others, culminating in His desire to see His children live in peace, in harmony, and in love. Jesus, an intermediary between our living God and humanity, said that we should also treat others the same way we would like to be treated. In this episode, the key word or even the theme of this message is love. God is good all the time, and so is Christ. Christ discourages self-hatred. The manifestation of love from one end to another is the signal of treating others well, because they are as important as you are.

The very best way to show love to your neighbours is to consider yourself in someone else's shoes, meaning being in someone's place or state. When you think of how you expect others to treat you, you must, in the same vein, think of how you should treat others. Do you expect friends, colleagues, parents, and contemporaries to accord you due respect? Then you should act in the same manner. The same way you expect others to show to you empathy, the same way you should show empathy to others. There must be fairness in life, for equity is equality. The legendary Sir Isaac Newton in his third law of motion said, "Action and reaction must be equal and opposite." Why then do you disrespect countless others, and you expect the same countless others to respect you? Isn't it an abnormal behaviour? Think about that and give it a serious thought.

The biblical quotation states, "Whoever claims to love God yet hates a brother or sister is a liar. For whoever does not love their brother and sister, whom they have seen, cannot love God. Anyone who loves God must also love their brother and sister." (1 John 4:20–21)

The truth of the matter is that, sometimes, it is very difficult to trust and, at the same, love your neighbours who have seriously offended you. Picture a difficult situation where someone has betrayed you. How can you love that individual who has spitefully dealt with you or caused extensive pain to you and your family, be it nuclear or extended? Love for such individual thus becomes difficult to evince. Yet you are instructed to do so, so that "you may be children of the Father in heaven; for He causes His sun to rise on the evil and the good" (Matthew 5:45). Notwithstanding this episode, Christ commands us to love our offenders, to the extent that we should even pray for them. Impossibility! Jesus says in Matthew 5:44, "But I say to you, love your enemies, bless those who curse you, do good to those who hate you, and pray for those who spitefully use you and persecute you" (NKJV).

The point here is that if we actually wish to be sons of God, we should cultivate the spirit of forgiveness. In addition, we should pray for our enemies, and the consequence of this prayer would be beneficial for those who always pray for their enemies. Let us therefore obey God and His precepts for our total benefit.

However, sometimes it is difficult to forgive others because there are some people who would never say sorry; and there are others who don't deserve forgiveness because they are not ready to change their behaviour; and there are still others who will continue to hurt us even when we try to forgive them; and there are still others who never think to make mistakes and so never ask for forgiveness. But God says in His word, "My dear child, forgive them" (Matthew 6:14–15). However, forgiving someone does not mean you have to open yourself to any further abuse. Developing a plan to protect your life is a wise decision you would ever make in your entire life. But in your heart, forgive your offenders.

Dear Christian, let us function in the full throttle of the power God has given to us. A significant portion of that power involves our forgiving nature. Failing to forgive one another, we cannot function in that power, and our prayers are never going to be answered. As

Christians, we are mostly ridiculed by the world because of our unforgiving nature. James, on the subject of prayers, tells Christians to "confess their sins to each other and pray for each other so that they may be healed" (James 5:16). On this account, to be healed, forgiveness is a prerequisite for receiving divine healing—from God.

Central to the above is the theme of love. Love is all that God wants from us, for He alone is love. Therefore, should we decide to become sons of God, we should love one another. For without love, we are "nothing" (1 Corinthians 13:2).

That God places a premium on love could not be underestimated. His demand to strengthen the need for love is put in the double commandment of love in loving both God and our neighbours as ourselves. Once we love, we should at the same time learn to forgive others. Avoid saying, "I forgive but never forget!" Unforgiving is ungodly! Forgiveness, Jesus said, is a golden rule. The Christian should not find it difficult to forgive, because God forgives those who offend Him. The Golden Rule is "Do to others what you want them to do to you."

In order to achieve this social status of love, we as human beings must recognise God's first greatest commandment, which reads, "Love the Lord your God with all your heart and with all your soul and with all your mind" (Matthew 22:37; Mark 12:30; Luke 10:27). To love God is to put Him first in everything. God must be your priority in everything you do. In the United States, their motto is "In God We Trust." That means God becomes first in everything they decide to do as a nation. But what do we see today? God is last in everything they do. As Christians, God should be the zenith of whatever thing we want to achieve. The Christian cannot love God and the world as the same (1 John 2:15).

"But God demonstrates His own love for us in this: While we were still sinners, Christ died for us" (Romans 5:8). Loving your neighbours and being hospitable should be the lifestyle of any ardent Christian. The story of the Good Samaritan is a classic example of showing love to one's neighbour. The question to ask is, "Who is your neighbour?"

Longman Dictionary of Contemporary English, sixth edition, defines neighbour as someone who lives next to you or near you. Neighbour could also mean someone or something that is next to another person or thing of the same type. Therefore one's spouse, one's children, a family member, or any other person apart from yourself could be your neighbour. People around your place of abode are all your neighbours. The rest of people from your village, other cities, regions, countries, and continents are equally one's neighbour.

Jesus advises that we should love our neighbours. Such neighbours could be any people from any part of the globe irrespective of their tribe or race. Consider the story of the Good Samaritan. The Jews and the Samaritans had been enemies for a long time. Prolonged mutual antagonism had existed between these two groups of people. When the Samaritan saw the injured Jew, the latter spent all his resources to treat the wounds of the Jew. This is the love Jesus of Nazareth is preaching. The Samaritan showed love to the Jew, though the two categories of people were "enemies". Here, love is portrayed as caring—caring for the well-being of a fellow human who is in need or in pain, who constitutes your neighbour. The Samaritan did not ask whether the wounded was a good man, religious, or rich. He did what a real man would do—help a fellow human being who was in need.

Possibly, there are a lot of things society can do now to show how best we can care for our neighbours who are in need. First, we can consider orphans and widows around us. In fact, there are countless orphans and widows worldwide, of whom some are very close to us, in our families or in our churches or in our communities, who may, one way or the other, need our assistance for their survival and possibly to give smiles to their faces. James chapter 1 verse 27 has this for his audience:

"Religion that God our Father accepts as pure and faultless is this: To look after orphans and widows in their distress and to keep oneself from being polluted by the world."

From the above scriptural verse, Christians are obligated to visit widows, especially the orphans to break up their suffering and make them live as though their wives or husbands and parents were living and taking good care of them. Imagine on their birthdays and anniversaries, parents or children could have given gifts to show their love for each other! In times of sorrow, still, wives or husbands or children would have been around to show their sympathy. The essential thing one could do is to visit the affected people and encourage them so that they may come out from their predicament; they should not come to beg from us.

"Jesus went through all the towns and villages, teaching in their synagogues, preaching the good news of the kingdom and healing every disease and sickness" (Matthew 9:35). The Bible makes us understand that everywhere Jesus went, He was doing good. If you consider yourself pious, manifest your piety to orphans and widows by "healing every disease and sickness" that affects them. Through your movement to these people, you are ministering to their needs.

A story is told of a retired Seventh-Day Adventist woman who had the desire to bring "healing" mercies to some AIDS orphans who didn't have adequate nutrition. She and her church started to feed the children in her community a solid meal six days a week. Starting with 50 children, by the close of 2012, this woman was serving 300 children per day. A pre-school was set later to cater for the educational needs of forty-five of those children. Soon, the church members started a skills-development programme for women who teach one another skills that help them earn a living (The Role of the Church in the Community #9 – page 6 of 6). This demonstration of love of Jesus shows how meeting the needs of people is so crucial for Christians. What is your church doing to meet the demands of the needy?

Constant caring for those inside your church is a powerful evangelistic strategy. You can also plan to serve people outside your church and your community. Radio France Internationale has a club called

"Le Club de Radio France Internationale" and is committed to bring smiles to the faces of orphans. On January 7, 2017, a presenter made it clear on air that the club is determined to give gifts to less-endowed children in Benin. This presentation was made during Yuletide. Here, the radio station in faraway France, focuses on meeting the needs of people of different races.

> "Theresa Kachindamoto, the senior chief in the Dedza District of Central Malawi, wields power over close to 900,000 people and she's not afraid to use her authority to help the women and girls in her district. In the past three years, she has annulled more than 850 child marriages, sent hundreds of young women back to school to continue their education, and made strides to abolish cleansing rituals that require girls as young as seven to go to sexual initiation camps. With more than half of Malawi's girls married before the age of 18." (2012 United Nations survey—and a consistently low ranking on the human development index)

If your church has a clear plan to minister to the needs of the people, it is very important that all church members develop a suitable plan to make this plan a reality. Some church members may be doctors, nurses, philanthropists, teachers, counsellors, lawyers, or psychologists, and they may belong to benevolent organisations.

In the case of natural disasters in the form of flooding, storms, tsunamis, hurricanes, and earthquakes, these church members can contribute something in cash and in kind to assist the affected people in one way or the other.

In Ghana, for example, the national organisation referred to as NADMO (National Disaster Management Organization) is ever ready to assist victims of flooding and those whose homes are usually ripped off during early rains in the country, especially during the months of March and April every year. Some members of some churches and communities donate relief items to such victims. Philanthropists at times even build temporary structures to accommodate these victims.

Apostle Paul, during his ministry in Athens, became aware of the needs of the people. He realised that Gentile worshippers believed in some kind of deity, because they had built an altar to an unknown God. Using polished language, Apostle Paul then tried to win these people to know the true God.

While meeting the needs of victims, you could as well win souls for Christ by using a strategy. Some of these people may not be of the same status as you are. But through meeting their demand, be it medical, social, or financial, you are likely to minister to them and win as well. Paul's strategy was to lead those Gentiles away from their idols to the living God and Jesus raised from the dead. In brief, by assessing the needs of the needy, Apostle Paul tried to help fulfil their needs; you can do likewise.

Showing love is not the sole responsibility of the church. Members of society should also be involved. The rich and the affluent in the community could also contribute their quota in the process of sharing love to one another. Brilliant students who need to pursue higher academic work could be helped. Especially young people with gifts or talents but without help to let their dreams come into reality could also be sponsored or coached. Consider a bumpkin, from tropical Africa who has passed his examination and has been offered a scholarship to pursue a medical course in the Western world but lacks money to purchase an airline ticket; what do we do? Such a brilliant student is an asset to society and therefore should be helped to go. The affluent should not use their money to go after prostitutes and throw wild parties. The Bible tells us that if anybody is of the world, he is not of the Father (1 John 2:15). Therefore, to be with the Father above, we should think about things above. Love for one another should be the order of all human beings.

Christ showed sympathy. Why not you if you profess to be pious? Loving your neighbour should be your goal, if not your priority. As pointed earlier, our neighbour is anyone we encounter who is in need.

Do not use your religion, tribe, or race as an excuse not to help some-one who most likely could never pay you back. It doesn't matter who a person is. The one in need is the one we should help. As Christians, we should do well to remove all barriers in connection with national-ity, race, or caste. All people are of one family by creation. God is our Father, and we are His children. Christ came to demolish every wall that set barriers between us—as children of God. His love is broad and deep. Therefore, whatever thing you do for a neighbour, don't expect reciprocity from him or her. Your reward is from heaven—from God (Revelations 22:12). God's mercy is extensive and measureless. It extends across all creation. God longs for everybody to follow His examples and become a going community—not content to rest on what we have. We are told to reach out to people with the good news of salvation to where people live, work, and play. Jesus, at this juncture, is telling us to show love and be kind to people we visit, even if they hate us. Jesus is trying to link us to the character of God Himself. "But love your enemies, do good to them, and lend to them without expect-ing to get anything back. Then your reward will be great, and you will be children of the Most High, because He is kind to the ungrateful and wicked. Be merciful, just as your Father is merciful" (Luke 6:35).

The beatitudes (Matthew 5–7) identify Christ's disciples. The Christian should cultivate them while journeying with Christ. Ultimately, after the resurrection of Jesus, during the ministry of His disciples, meeting the churches and teaching them about the Doctrine of Christ, the people living in Antioch, who were not follow-ers of Christ, were able to recognise that the disciples had been with Christ (See Acts 11:19–26). This was as a result of their beatitudinal virtues exhibited while doing the work of God. On that account, the Christian, who is a disciple of Christ, needs to be identified by the beatitudes.

The sinner, after being converted into Christ, is committed to change. But the Christian himself could be an impediment to change. Even though the Holy Spirit is the agent of change, the Christian plays a vital role in the transformation process.

"Loving the Lord your God with all your heart and with all your mind and with all your strength; and loving your neighbour as your-self" is the summary of the New Testament worship. Don Bjork of Worldteam points out that the great commission was given to wor-shipping people. Loving God and loving your neighbour is what God requires.

The Christian needs to cultivate the spirit of love. I squirm to sug-gest that we've set ourselves up for ridicule, because we have shifted from one of the purposes of our creation—to live as social beings. Instead of loving ourselves, we are hating ourselves—hatred, selfish-ness, bickering, greed, and many other evil acts have surfaced the order of human life. If we are to love only those who love us, and pray for only those who pray for us, and do good to only those who do good to us, then someone out there needs to feel sorry for us. Jesus said to his audience: "If you love those who love you, what reward will you get? Are not even tax collectors doing that? And if you greet only your own people, what are you doing more than others? Do not even pagans do that?" (Matthew 5:46–47). In verse 48, He concluded by saying, "Be perfect, therefore, as your heavenly Father is perfect."

"Love is patient, love is kind. It does not envy, it does not boast, it is not proud. It does not dishonour others, it is not self-seeking, it is not easily angered, it keeps no record of wrongs. Love does not delight in evil but rejoices with the truth. It always protects, always trusts, always hopes, always perseveres. Love never fails. But where there are prophecies, they will cease; where there are tongues, they will be stilled; where there is knowledge, it will pass away." (1 Corinthians 13:4–8)

Love is patient. It never gets tired of others—husband, children, in-laws, friends, families, and even strangers. Patient according to the Oxford Dictionary is able to accept or tolerate delays, problems, or suffering without becoming annoyed or anxious.

Are you impatient? If yes, then know that, patience is a virtue. Cultivate it. Always ask yourself, "Why do I have to be patient with others?" and answer, "Because God was and is still patient with me.

He was so patient with me that He sent His Son Jesus to die for my sins, and He is still patient with me when I don't do what He requires from me. And if I love God, I will also be patient with others."

Love is kind. Four years ago in Italy, a man left his local church because he wanted to help his elder brother, who was a pastor in another church. Mr. Sam, that's the man's name; he was one of the founding members of his church in Italy, in the 90s, and a very dedicated Christian. He was also the church's bus driver. He was known by almost everyone in the church. But the worst thing was that when he left the church, no one called Mr. Sam on the phone to say hi, and no one visited his home even when her wife gave birth to a child. He felt lonely and being rejected by the people. Finally, he concluded that the people in his previous church did not love him. What do you say about that?

Do you show kindness only to those who do good to you? Do you talk only to the rich or the affluent in the society? Are you kind to others? How often do you say thank you to the public bus driver? When was the last time you ever spoke kind words to someone who was going through suffering?

Kindness is a virtue. Cultivate it. Always ask yourself, "Why do I have to be kind to others?" and answer, "Because God was and is still kind to me. He gives me daily bread. He clothes me. He opens the right doors for me. He uses music to soothe my soul. He communicates with me through prayers. And if I love God, I will also be kind to others."

Love does not envy. The Greek term for the verb "envy" means to have a warmth of feeling for or against. In 1 Corinthians 13:4, Apostle Paul uses the word envy in the negative connotation. It is contrary to the nature of love: "Love is not jealous" or "love does not envy." So when the Bible says that "love does not envy," it means that the Christian should not be unhappy about, or wish the downfall of others. Love rejoices with the welfare of others.

The simple explanation to "**love does not boast**" is that those who reflect the nature of God do not think too highly of themselves. They are not arrogant. They esteem others better than themselves (Philippians 2:3). They know that everything they possess and are able to do is by the grace of God. When they want to boast about themselves, they do so in Christ (1 Corinthians 1:31; 2 Corinthians 10:17).

Love is not proud is similar to the expression "love does not boast." But there is a difference. Studies tell us that pride is the mind-set and attitude, while boasting is the speech and conduct. The opposite of pride is humility. Love is humble. Proverbs 16:18 says, "Pride goes before destruction, a haughty spirit before a fall."

Love does not dishonour others. God imbued His children with His love. His love does not dishonour God and others. Love is not humiliating. Love is encouraging. If you love your neighbours, you show them honour—you respect, consider their opinions and feelings, and cherish their efforts. If you love your neighbours, you do not belittle them.

Another version uses, "Love is not rude." Rude is showing a lack of respect for other people and their feelings. Another word for rude is impolite. You could be rude to anyone—to your parents, pastor, friends, or a stranger. Need an example? Ted, a 13 year old boy, walked into a restaurant full of adults and screamed, "I can chew bones. Raise your hand, if you can." Love does not behave indecently. Love has good manners.

At the age of 7, my late grandmother, Elizabeth Abbrey, taught me courtesy for boys and girls. I was taught how to say please, thank you, and sorry. I was also taught to leave my seat for the elderly parent. Today, things have changed from good to bad—it is common to see young people exchanging words with adults, which is so bad! As a Christian youth, show respect to everyone, especially the elderly people in our society.

In order to please the Sovereign God, the Christian should eschew rudeness. Being rude tarnishes your image. Again, love is not rude and does not dishonour others.

Love is not self-seeking. Love is not selfish. It does not pursue a personal ambition. Love seeks the welfare of others. Love gives. I quote one of my favourite poems:

A bell is not a bell until you ring it
A song is not a song until you sing it.
Love in your heart is not put there to stay,
Love is not love until you give it away.
(Oscar Hammerstein II, an American writer, theatrical pro-
ducer, and (usually uncredited) theatre director of musicals
for almost forty years).

Reciting and examining the poem, you come to understand that love is not selfish. Love gives. Going back to the last line, it reads, "Love is not love until you give it away." Apostle Paul puts it this way: "If I speak with the tongues of men and of angels, but do not have love, I am like a resounding gong or a clanging cymbal." (1 Corinthians 13:1). Other versions use, "I am nothing." Thus without love, we are nothing to please God.

Love is not easily angered. There are a lot of people who get angry about petty things. Anger itself is not sinful, but it can quickly lead to sinful expressions. Apostle Paul wrote to the Ephesians, "In your anger do not sin: Do not let the sun go down while you are still angry, and do not give the devil a foothold" (Ephesians 4:26–27). Love does not take offence. Love will guide us in the proper way to handle our anger.

Beloved, God is not tired with you and me. He continues to love us when we mess up everything. Jesus suffered on earth to experience our pain when we go through sufferings. Let's stay faithful to one another. Someone said: "Pure heart is the greatest temple in the world." We may come from different ethnic backgrounds or families, but we as Christians are from one big family called the Family of God, and the Head of that family is God Himself. Let us love one another. Without love, we are nobody (1 Corinthians 13:1). The Golden Rule is "Do to others what you would want them to do to you."

5
The New Birth
(Jesus and Nicodemus)

A LOT IS always said, spoken, and written about Jesus. If we were to continue in this piece of writing, it would constitute not only garbage but also repetition of words, which in consequence would turn into a cliché. The question "Who is Jesus?" at this time of earth's history should not be a philosophical or a sociological gimmick. It gets to the sub-consciousness of human beings who are praised to know about what eternity holds for them.

Today, many people admire the works of Jesus, honour His words, admire His patience, advocate His non-violent nature, uphold His decisiveness, and categorise Him as a good man and leader who tried to set things right. Equity and equality are His fair play, especially where there was injustice. He was ever prepared to offer healing where there was sickness. He was also quick to bring comfort where there was misery.

The Gospel according to Saint Luke places the story of Jesus in history as real people and real times in order to discuss any idea of mythology with his writing. Readers of Luke must stand in awe and wonder at the fact that Jesus is real and that through Him God has invaded history with the "Saviour, who is Christ the Lord" (Luke 2:11).

Indeed, Jesus could well earn the name of a revolutionist, a great leader, and a psychologist who could probe into the depths of one's soul. He was all these and so much more. Consider Jesus as "Son of man" and "Son of God" (See Luke 22:67–70). The use of "Son of man" in Luke provides insight into the nature, mission, and destiny of the incarnate Jesus. Also, the expression is used to describe His messianic role, redemptive as well as the One Who returns to the earth to reward His saints and to wrap up the great controversy (See Luke 9:26, 36; 22:69). In short, the use of "Son of Man" bears multiple aspects of what He came to do and what He has accomplished and will accomplish for us in the plan of salvation.

When Christ came to the earth, humanity seemed to be fast reaching its lowest point. Life had become false and artificial. Truth, honour, integrity, confidence, and compassion were departing from the face of the earth. The common people were regarded as beasts and nonentities. Wealth and power and self-indulgence were sought as the highest good. Spiritual death characterised the age. It is upon this that Christ came to the earth to teach the right way of life and to earn salvation of their lives.

While interacting and healing humanity, Nicodemus fell into the orbit of Jesus's ministry. Nicodemus, a ruler of the Jews, referred Jesus as "Rabbi," meaning a teacher (See John 3:2). Jesus had a night time rendezvous with Nicodemus. Jesus did not revere this Nicodemus as a social elite during that era. Jesus recognised that wealthy, well-positioned, famous people needed salvation and that financial prosperity could not supply peace, happiness, and meaningful relationships.

Having realised that the wealthy could easily be lonelier and emptier than the poorest Christian, Jesus interacted with Nicodemus.

What might be interesting is that Nicodemus met Jesus in secret. Nicodemus had witnessed God's power and authority as revealed through Jesus's ministry. He decided to meet Jesus. Jesus the rabbi could have refused this secret venture proposed by Nicodemus, but He was unwilling that any should perish. He readily accepted this opportunity to bring Nicodemus closer to God and His Kingdom.

Nicodemus's poverty was not financial or material but spiritual. Nicodemus was extremely rich and had a high social standing. Unfortunately, spiritually, he was zero. In spite of his persistent rebellion against conversion to Christianity, Jesus persisted, presenting to Nicodemus with the eternal choice between judgement and salvation. Initially, Nicodemus refused to accept Christ's invitation. This was due to the fact that he feared being ridiculed by his fellow men. Nicodemus's interview with Jesus had failed. What next? The spiritual seed started to germinate slowly in his heart.

According to Mrs. Ellen G. White in *The Desire of Ages*, page 177, "After the Lord's ascension, when the disciples were scattered by persecution, Nicodemus came boldly to the front. He employed his wealth in sustaining the infant church that the Jews had expected to be blotted out at the death of Christ. In the time of peril, he (Nicodemus) who had been so cautious and questioning was firm as a rock, encouraging the faith of the disciples, and furnishing means to carry forward the work of the gospel. He was scorned and persecuted by those who had paid him reverence in other days. He became poor in his world's good; yet he faltered not in the faith which had its beginning in that night conference with Jesus."

Nicodemus's conversion had played a significant role in maintaining an infant Christian movement. The Kingdom of God consists of honest-hearted people from every social class. The Christian should not be intimidated by wealthy people but should fearlessly proclaim God's revelation that they may be saved.

It must be emphasised that during the dialogue Jesus said, "I tell you the truth, no one can see the Kingdom of God unless he is born again" (John 3:3). This statement paved the way for Nicodemus to ask Jesus, "How can a man be born when he is old?" Jesus answered, "I tell you the truth, no one can enter the Kingdom of God unless he is born of water and the spirit" (John 3:5). Jesus says, "You must be born again," and, "You must be born of water and the spirit." This drama allows both the speaker and his interlocutor to address each other.

Such a situation brings an understanding between the two. And that was what Jesus did. You are advised to minister in the same manner. Jesus did that, and Nicodemus became a born-again Christian.

What does it mean to be born again? The original Greek word translates "again" more commonly from above, thus heaven. The issue of born-again in this regard is not physical but spiritual. Jesus is reported as saying, "Born of water and the spirit" (John 3:5). That water, referred to as living water, is the Holy Spirit (John 7:37–39). It is the ministry of the Holy Spirit to bring life and light into the world through the life of the Christian. The Spirit lives in the Christian because the body of the Christian is the temple of the Holy Spirit (See 1 Corinthians 3:16; 6:19). In addition, after Jesus had spoken with the Samaritan woman at the well of Jacob, she said, "Sir, give me this water so that I won't get thirsty and have to keep coming here to draw water" (John 4:15). The woman didn't know that Jesus was talking about Himself. Jesus is the living water. The living water gives eternal life. And Jesus is the only one who gives life. At verse 15, Jesus calls the life He gives "eternal life."

We should not forget that the Holy Spirit is the enabler for spiritual birth. Jesus says, "No one can come to me unless the Father who sent me draws him…" (John 6:44). Thus the Spirit is active in time of repentance. Nicodemus knows God, but he doesn't know Jesus the Messiah, Who is the way to the Father (God). Though a religious leader, Nicodemus needed a change of heart to become a born-again Christian.

Ezekiel 36:26–27 gives a vivid description of how God was willing to renew the life of humanity by putting in them a new spirit and heart. Cruelty has enslaved humanity. The Almighty God loves humans and, in consequence, orders Ezekiel to alert humanity that He is prepared to give "a new heart and put a new spirit in him." God sends someone, and the messenger reaches the sinner with the gospel. A heart of stone finds it extremely difficult to repent. While receiving the gospel, the Holy Spirit explains Christ's message to the sinner that Jesus died for the world. Finally, the sinner is convinced. Repentance sets in. The sinner is now repented, and his or her sins are forgiven. The sinner now becomes born-again and a son or daughter of God (John 1:12–13).

2 Corinthians 7:10 has it that "Godly sorrow brings repentance that leads to salvation and leaves no regret, but worldly sorrow brings death." Apostle Paul, at this juncture emphasises genuine repentance, which brings salvation, while the opposite leads to total destruction.

Following this argument, the sinner becomes born-again. His sins are forgiven, and he or she has become a new creation, as recorded in 2 Corinthians 5:17, "Therefore, if anyone is in Christ, he is a new creation; old things have passed away; behold all things have become new" (NKJV).

As soon as one is born again, that person becomes a child of God, born not of natural descent, nor of human decision, nor out of wedlock, but born of God (See John 1:12–13). In order to be a Christian, you need to ask for forgiveness of your sins by a simple confession. Paul says, "If you declare with your mouth, "Jesus is Lord" and believe in your heart that God raised Him from the dead, you will be saved. For it is with the heart that you believe and are justified, and it is with the mouth that you profess and are saved" (Romans 10:9).

Change and Become Like Little Children.

Many churches of today place a premium on ministering to the adult population rather than that of children. A lot of such churches direct their greatest resources towards the adult population. This situation was the same during Jesus's era when almost all the churches underestimated the value of children's ministry. Jesus rejected that attitude and made room for children, even giving them priority. We are advised to do the same. Why do we need to do the same?

There exists a unique genuineness within children that Christ frequently appealed to when illustrating His kingdom. Their genuineness, humility, love, and innocence capture the essence of Christian living. It is true that children never leave their childlike dependency behind. When properly educated, children may carry their trusting innocence into adulthood. As a result of this positive tendency among children, we should do all things possible to instil in children the fear of God and His love. Such education may expose your children to love, kindness, compassion, and care they should exhibit as they grow into adulthood. This is the best way to discipline children to live to exhibit the love of God to their hearers. Consider the text below:

> And he said: "Truly I tell you, unless you change and become like little children, you will never enter the Kingdom of heaven. Therefore, whoever takes the lowly position of this child is the greatest in the Kingdom of heaven. And whoever welcomes one such child in my name welcomes me." (Matthew 18:3–5 NKJV)

In answer to the riddle posed by the apostles, Jesus was emphatic that unless one becomes like a child, one cannot inherit the Kingdom of heaven/God. Jesus's answer, though small, is as powerful as a bomb blast killing billions of people at a time. What a powerful object lesson from Christ!

Here, Jesus is teaching His disciples to act in a puerile manner in the traditional sense. They should exhibit and cultivate the spirit of humility, genuineness, goodness, forgiveness, and compassion in all their endeavours, and this would eventually lead them into eternal life. Jesus says, "Blessed are the meek, for they will inherit the earth" (Mathew 5:5). Meekness in spirit is of great value before God (See 1 Peter 3:4).

We Are Saved by Grace and Faith in Jesus.

We are saved by grace. Grace is receiving something you do not deserve. In other words, Grace is unmerited favour. According to scriptures, you were condemned to death (See Romans 3:23), but Christ paid the price by taking your place (Romans 5:8). You had unmerited favour from God through Jesus, Who sacrificed His life to die a shameful death in your place on the cross. He took your burden of sins away. Jesus died because of a sinner like you. On the Calvary's cross Jesus suffered for you. What a manifestation of love!

God's will is not for anyone to perish (See Matthew 18:14). The will of God is to save every sinner through Jesus. The Bible says, "As Jesus approached Jericho, a blind man was sitting by the roadside begging. When he heard the crowd going by, he asked what was happening. They told him, "Jesus of Nazareth is passing by. He called out, "Jesus, Son of David, have mercy on me!" (Luke 18:35–38). The story continues in verse 40 that, "Jesus stopped and ordered the man to be brought to him. When he came near, Jesus asked him, "What do you want me to do for you" "Lord, I want to see," he replied (in verse 41). Jesus said to him, "Receive your sight; your faith has healed you" (in verse 42). Immediately he received his sight and followed Jesus, praising God (in verse 43). Indeed, God's is merciful to all!

Repeatedly, faith in Christ is what saves and not our works; it is God's grace (Ephesians 2:8–9). In Acts 16:30–31, it says, "He then brought them out and asked, 'Sirs, what must I do to be saved?' They replied, 'Believe in the Lord Jesus, and you will be saved—you and your household.'"

For our faith to lead to salvation, it must be centred in Christ. We should trust and follow Jesus wherever He may lead us. To follow Jesus is to follow His teachings and His way of life.

Again, to have faith in Jesus is to reject sin. The Bible tells us that God is holy and hates sin (1 Peter 1:16). "For the wages of sin is death, but the gift of God is eternal life in Christ Jesus our Lord" (Romans 6:23).

To have faith in Jesus is to fully trust Him. When you have faith in Jesus, it means that you believe who Jesus is. That means you believe Jesus is God. John 14:6 tells us that Jesus is the only way, the only truth, and the only life. "Salvation is found in no one else, for there is no other name under heaven given to mankind by which we must be saved" (Acts 4:12).

To have faith in Jesus is to put Him first in everything. Jesus becomes the centre of your life. Is Jesus the centre of your life?

Jesus Is the Truth.

Scholars, especially philosophers have argued for centuries that there is no absolute truth and that all truths are a matter of opinion. And so when you are asked to talk about absolute truth, you should say what is in your mind. Listen to what Jesus Himself told Thomas (in John 14:6): "I am the Way, the Truth and the Life. No one comes to the Father except through me." Who is the truth, according to John the writer? Jesus is "the truth." He spoke and lived in harmony with the truth, and he fulfilled all prophecies (See 2 Corinthians 1:20).

Knowing God vs. Knowing about God.

Knowing God is not the same as knowing about God. Let's say that you are a huge fun of a gospel singer, like Daniel Adomako. Daniel Adomako is an Italian-based Ghanaian gospel artiste. Let's say that you know all facts about his life: When he was born, the name of his parents, his favourite food, his hobbies, his mentors, and so on. Let's say you've watched all his favourite movies, listened to all his favourite songs, and read all his favourite books. You still don't know Daniel. This is what some define in psychology as *impersonal knowledge.*

Knowing someone is coming to experience the personal life of that person. Let's say that you know your friends because they actively share personal information with you. Not only that, but also they spend time with you. This is what some define in psychology as *personal knowledge.* Likewise in the Christian context, knowing God is to enter into a relationship with Him. John 15:9 says, "As the Father has loved me, so I have loved you. Now remain in my love." We, human beings, were created to have a fellowship with God but because of our sins, we chose to go on our own way, and that fellowship was broken. But thanks be to Jesus for mending that broken walls between us and God. Now we still have that relationship only when we give God our hearts.

Going back to the story of Jesus and Nicodemus, Jesus said to him, "No one can see the Kingdom of God unless he is born again" (John 3:3). That means, knowing about God is not enough. A person needs to be born again, because it is one of the criteria to enter into the Kingdom of God.

Being born again is necessary. It gives one:

- A new creation (2 Corinthians 5:17)
- A new life (Romans 6:4–11)
- The power to overcome the world (1 John 5:4–5)
- Delivers one from sin's enslavement (1 John 3:4–9, 5:19)
- Stirs one to be righteous (1 John 2:9)
- Stirs one to love others (1 John 4:7–11)

Baptism is an obedience step to salvation, and no one can skip baptism after repentance. Thus baptism is an obligation for the one who believes. Immediately one has repented, the next step is to be baptised. From Christ's example, it is inferred that baptism is essential and mandatory. From the Bible, we read that Jesus travelled on foot from Nazareth to the Jordan River to be baptised by John (See Matthew 3:13).

Truthfully, the Christian should be baptised as Christ said to His apostles, "Baptise them in the name of the Father, and of the Son, and of the Holy Spirit" (Matthew 28:19). Baptism by immersion should not be taken for granted. In recording the baptism of Jesus, He, being the Saviour, did not refuse to be baptised; He allowed Himself to be baptised by John so that generations would follow the same pattern of baptism. We must obey the instructions of our Lord Jesus by baptising everyone who believes in Him.

Why baptism? Baptism illustrates the believer's identification with Christ's death, burial, and resurrection. In simplicity, when we are baptised, we die, we are buried, and we are resurrected with Christ. It means our sins are buried, and we resurrect with a new life as if we live sinlessly as Christ lived. Read Romans 6:3–4 for more details.

The Christian is baptised into Christ, and no one else. Apostle Paul says that there is no name on earth for which we must be saved (See Acts 4:12). Salvation comes through faith in Christ, and it is only Christ who saves.

Dear Christian, we live in a world divided over religion. The Christian needs to avoid any form of argument that leads to hatred. Instead, we are advised to be kind and loving to others irrespective of their perception, religion, beliefs, practices, and socio-political differences. We are to remain open to the possibility that we may be wrong on some matters. The same way we expect others to keep an open mind, the same way our hearers expect us to keep an open mind.

Nonetheless, to know the truth about life and Christianity, we must listen to what Jesus teaches. When it comes to baptism, Jesus left Nazareth and came to the Jordan River to be baptised by John. Baptism is an integral part of the Gospel. Moreover, it is a spiritual step after repentance.

The Bible says that Philip and the Ethiopian nobleman were travelling from Jerusalem in the nobleman's chariot. When Philip taught the Ethiopian eunuch, "they both Philip and the eunuch, and Philip baptised him" (Acts 8:38). Per Jesus's example, the disciples did for others what John had done for Him. Another example is Cornelius and his household (See Acts 10; 11:1–18).

When it comes to infants, Christ clearly pictured baptism as the consequence of an informed choice made by persons who are capable of making decisions. Anyone who thus responds to Christ's invitation is the one who has been preached to or taught, is convicted of his or her sins, and makes a genuine decision to adhere to Christ, and as a result of that, this person is baptised. Before baptism, the sinner, who is now born again, must be taught about the needfulness of his or her salvation.

There is nowhere in the Bible anyone is baptised before that person is taught. This means that the sinner is taught before baptism takes place. And at this stage, we all believe that children or infants are not fully matured to make personal decisions for themselves. Therefore, children or infants should not be baptised until they are grown to a certain stage where they are able to make personal decisions. Then they are able to ask to be baptised.

To conclude, are you born again? Have you been baptised? Changed lives show the fruits of repentance. Christ's words to His disciples are "to preach and to baptise and to teach everything He has said." This means that after we have been baptised in water, there is one more thing for us to do—we should learn more about Jesus. We should learn more of His love.

6
Missiological Insight
(Making Disciples for Christ)

CHRISTIANS HAVE A duty to work for Christ. We are under a heavy obligation to carry the message of Christ across the waves to the ends of the world. The idea of segregation should be discarded when sending the gospel message across. Racial discrimination and other barriers preventing the Christian to do the will of the Master are strictly prohibited. The instruction of Christ is that we, as Christians, should go and make disciples for Him. In the same vein, Christians should do well to preach the Gospel of Christ, and after their audience have accepted the Word of God, the next sequence is that we should baptise them. This is what is referred to in Christianity as God's Great Commission. First, let us look at who a disciple is.

In its etymological sense, disciple originates from the Greek word "mathetes," meaning "learner," "apprentice," or "adherent." It depicts a person whose mind is set on a purpose. In the biblical sense, a disciple is used mostly of Jesus's disciples, especially in the Gospel of the New Testament. Disciple could also mean "an apprentice or pupil attached to a teacher or movement; whose allegiance is to instruction and commitments of the teacher or movement" (*Harper's Bible Dictionary*, edited by Paul J. Achtemier [San Francisco: Harper and Row, 1985], 222). This means that an apprentice should be guided by a teacher, and there cannot be an apprentice without an instructor. Discipleship therefore involves willingness to obey Christ's commands and make commitments. This explanation follows the fact that a disciple should automatically be a disciplined person wishing to follow or obey the commands of his or her master.

In the Bible, Jesus, the Son of God, is the pivot and fulcrum of our discipleship. It is only through Jesus that we owe allegiance and commitment to God. Anything beyond that reduces us from being a disciple. In other words, to be a good disciple, one should look to Jesus and learn His life and ministry.

The word discipleship connotes historical and personal perspectives. In the historical context, discipleship refers to the encounter between Christ Jesus, the Master Teacher, and His followers, known as disciples. At the nucleus, it referred to those who had a close and special affiliation with the Rabbi, Jesus Christ the Messiah. On the personal level, discipleship refers to the interaction that occurs between Christ Jesus, the transformed individual, and the world. Discipleship sums up to an intimate relationship between Jesus and His followers.

Jesus is the centre or the core of God's mission. He came into the world in a human form to offer salvation to sinners. In fact, He says: "I am the Way, the Truth and the Life (John 14:6a). Jesus affirms that with Him, the time for great deliverance from the kingdom of darkness to the kingdom of Light has come. He concludes: "The people living in darkness have seen a great light; on those living in the land of the shadow of death, a light has shown" (Matthew 4:16).

To become a disciple is the focus of this chapter. In most instances in the New Testament, disciples were chosen. This means that those disciples were chosen by Master Jesus Himself, and the chosen people responded to the call. In this sense, one doesn't become or make himself or herself a disciple. Becoming a disciple involves a divine initiative. And that's why Jesus says, "No one can come to me unless the

Father who sent me draws them." (John 6:44). In fact, discipleship is a work of grace so that we cannot become boastful. Christ extends the call for us, and He persuades us for acceptance.

An entry point to discipleship is the absolute willingness for the called to respond to a call. It is a divine invitation, and therefore, one should succumb oneself favourably to the call thrown by the Lord Jesus. In addition to this, willingness has to be based on something concrete, on something the disciple sees as valuable—faith should be the answer. The third requirement of discipleship is a natural outgrowth of the two mentioned. Willingness to follow and to believe must lead to a positive response, or there could be no discipleship.

A positive response and willingness to follow are ineffective unless put into active reality through obedience, an offshoot of discipline. Jesus invited each person initially called to follow Him, and they did so immediately. This means that the disciples were obedient and that obedience was a requirement for discipleship. It was amazing that after the acceptance of the call, all members had to break with the past, for it is said that "Therefore if anyone is in Christ, he is a new creation; old things have passed away; behold all things have become new" (2 Corinthians 5:17 NKJV). The disciples left their jobs, families, and possessions to follow Jesus. This is because they were prepared to deny themselves and follow their Master.

The reality of following Jesus was a call to a life of community and fellowship. Jesus and the disciples had a close relationship. In John 15:9, Jesus compared their relationship with that between Him and His Father. He calls on His disciples to abide in His love, further strengthening this idea of our need to be closer to the Master, learning from Him and becoming like Him. Mark 3:13 says that the disciples were called "to be with Him." It is certainly true that it is impossible for a disciple to be with Jesus and not learn from Him or be inspired to be like Him.

Jesus involved His disciples in every aspect of His ministry. When He sent them out to preach and teach, they did so with confidence because of what they had seen Him do, starting with His first miracle at Cana. So they would have heard Jesus's mother turning to tell her Son there was no wine. They saw her tell the servants to do as her Son instructed. The disciples must have watched with curiosity as Jesus told the servants to fill the six pots with water and then with growing amazement as He told them to take the water pots to the one in charge of the feast. The disciples were indeed surprised when water was turned into wine. This was the first miracle performed by Jesus.

Jesus, from the outset of His ministry, had disciples. He appeared to be a disciple-gathering teacher in the tradition of Greek and Jewish teachers. There were also points of contact with John the Baptist since John baptised Him in preparation for His mission. Jesus also had disciples who followed Him everywhere, who listened to His teachings and imitated Him. Jesus's call was for the love of God and a promise of eternal life. That's why today, many people accept Him so that in the end, salvation will be theirs.

Acts of discipleship during Jesus's era, that is, the first calls, spread like a wildfire. Andrew heard John speak about the Messiah and agreed to follow Jesus the Lamb of God. Next, Andrew told his brother Peter of his experience and brought him to Christ, and Peter became a follower as well. In the same way, today, when we hear the truth about Jesus, we make a commitment to follow Him and then tell others about Him. This action is repeated day by day, all over the world. Matthew and Mark also followed Jesus through His first calling. As soon as they were called, they dropped anchor their nets and followed Jesus. This explains the fact that Jesus demands the whole heart of the called. We should surrender to Him. We should abandon all earthly things that would serve as a bait to lure us into the kingdom of the devil. What is worse, those things we cling to become the hooks the devil uses to wean us away from Christ completely; we should be careful about that. We should follow any instructions given to us by Christ. James, John, the sons of Zebedee, and Simon, also known as Peter, followed Christ's instruction, and they had a large catch of fish. And Jesus said to Simon, "Do not be afraid. From now on you will catch men" (Luke 5:10 NKJV). This prophecy was fulfilled after the ascension of Jesus into the heavens (See Acts 2:31).

The call of Matthew's story is so fascinating. Matthew was considered as extortionist, a robber, who defrauded his own countrymen. Despite his reputation as a bad man in his society, Jesus called him to be a disciple and later an apostle. Jesus gives salvation to everybody irrespective of one's nature. Jesus speaks of the universality of salvation He brought. This tells us that Christ's invitation is for everyone.

Discipleship presupposes a rebirth that unites one with the heavenly realm and opens one up to the constant working of the Holy Spirit. We need to be filled with the Holy Spirit. The power of the Holy Spirit enables us to preach the Gospel of Christ with the anointing and strength and power without fear or persuasion. The Acts of Apostles acknowledges the fact that "when the Holy Spirit comes upon us, we shall receive power, and we shall be witnesses to Jesus (Acts 1:8). When the Holy Spirit came upon Peter, he preached without fear. On that same day, after his preaching, three thousand souls were saved (See Acts 2:14–42). When we allow ourselves to be led by the Holy Spirit, He will lead us to where we cannot go.

Whenever Christians are led by the Holy Spirit, souls will listen to our messages and come to the Lord Jesus. Our legitimate duty is to share the Word with others that Jesus died for their sins. As to how your audience will absorb your message is the absolute will of the Holy Spirit to accomplish the task—He convicts sinners. Therefore, we should not be afraid to move, to do, if possible, house-to-house or personal evangelism.

Making disciples might require us to do strange things: Eat or drink strange mixtures and be all things to all people in order to win some for Christ. This is the call and challenge of discipleship, especially as the Gospel of Christ goes around the world and into cultures some-times radically different from our own. Christ breaks down all bar-riers. Not only did Christ create all humanity, He also died for all humanity, regardless of race, nationality, or ethnic origin. It was no wonder, then, that when Jesus was here on earth, He ministered not just to the Jews but to non-Jews as well. Though Paul is understood to be the apostle to Gentiles, Jesus was already witnessing to them when He was in the flesh. The Samaritan woman at the well left her water pots and went to invite the villagers to meet Jesus after He had told her everything she ever did. As a result, many villagers believed in Jesus, simply because that woman gave testimony about Him.

The story of the ten lepers (Luke 17:11–16) also speaks to Jesus's work for Samaritans. The tenth leper went and showed his grate-fulness for what the Lord Jesus had done for Him. Jesus told this Samaritan that his faith had saved him not only physically but also spiritually. Despite knowing him to be a Samaritan and a foreigner, Jesus did not discriminate against him but rewarded his faith. These encounters show that Jesus did not conform to prejudices of His time. Jesus's love was demonstrated to all those who had personal contact with Him irrespective of their family, educational, political, social, or cultural background.

The story of Cornelius is another example of doing away with ethnicity when taking up discipleship. Acts 10 mentions this Roman official of Cornelius. As a God fearer and centurion, Cornelius was generous to the needy and prayed earnestly to God. God sent an angel to inform him of the acceptance of his gifts and prayers and sent him in search of Peter. Apostle Peter went away to his home, contrary to Jewish scruples, and was even reprimanded for it. But God told him not to call common or unclean those, like Cornelius, whom He had cleansed. As Peter preached to Cornelius's assembled household (See Acts 10:44–48), the Holy Spirit interrupted him with the Gentile Pentecost to the amazement of his Jewish companions. We should be careful not to allow any cultural, educational, or social influences characterise our discipleship to the principles of Christ to hinder us from living to the fullest the profession we claim for ourselves.

To prepare for discipleship, one needs to be called. And this invitation call is a prerogative of the Master. Jesus extends the call, and we respond to that call. A disciple, as we know, is a learner, who follows his or her master. While both a disciple and an apostle are students, an apostle receives additional training or instructions or teachings to be sent forth as an ambassador of the Master.

Jesus appointed the twelve so that they might be with Him and that He might send them out to preach. Matthew says, "He gave them authority to drive out evil spirits and to heal every disease and sickness" (Matthew 10:1). He chose them to provide workers to assist in caring for large throngs that flocked wherever He went.

When Jesus called the first disciples, He said that He would make them fishers of men (Matthew 4:19). They were to go and draw men to Christ, making them disciples, who would then go and draw others to Jesus. But before they could be effective soul winners, the disciples spent some time with Jesus, observing and learning just what it was that they were called to do. They were to render services to humanity as directed by the Master (Jesus). The word "service" could be an acronym that is expanded below:

S = Sensitivity
E = Expertise
R = Responsibility
V = Value
I = Intelligence
C = Commitment
E = Excellence

The above acronym explains the fact that before beginning discipleship, one ought to possess the above qualities. By so doing, one will be worthy of emulation. We must emphasise that discipleship is a function of every Christian. Those who choose to follow Christ have been called not only to follow but also to serve. As we witness to others about the good news of the Gospel that Christ came to save them, we must also tell them of their calling to become Disciples of Christ. Discipleship is an experience. Experience from where? From the Master. In our case, from Jesus. Being able to recite the Bible is not enough, knowing Bible doctrines is not enough, and giving huge sums of money to support your church is not enough. All that we need as our passport to evangelism is personal contact with Christ and possession of a changed life, referred to as being "born again". Also, humility should be a hallmark of a disciple. Jesus said that we must be humble just like children. Children cannot survive on their own; we cannot survive our discipleship without Christ. As Christians, we should be equipped with constant prayers and the principles of faith. These attributes of children would help us (Christians) succeed in all our endeavours.

Learning the culture, tradition and language of the area of target for soul-winning is necessary. It is also advisable for the disciple or the church or the missionary to investigate the cultural practices and traditions of the nation or tribe or community in order to make evangelism effective.

Also, there are so many important ways to create evangelistic activities with music. Music plays a vital role in evangelism, because songs speak to people. We must sing to praise and worship God. On the other hand, some Christians believe that music would win young people to Christ. That is false! To be blunt, sinners come to Christ Jesus not by the use of human instrumentalities, but rather by the conviction of the Holy Spirit after the message of Christ has been preached. The Christian should also know that some of the so-called gospel music may be referred to as "Christian," but it is not, simply because the rhythmic pattern of most of the songs doesn't suit gospel music; such pattern sounds worldly. However, the lyrics in a gospel song can save the sinner. What matters most is that, it is the Holy

Spirit Who convicts the sinner to come to Christ and make Him Lord and Saviour. The end of the matter is that let us create evangelistic activities with music.

At this stage, let's consider mentorship. Deliberating on the mission's work of Jesus with a Christian brother, we came to the realisation that Jesus and the apostles preached effectively in the Arab world, making sure that the Gospel had reached the people. But after the death of Jesus and the apostles, consider today, it seems Jesus and the apostles never preached in those areas. But we read from the Bible that Jesus Himself took time to invest in those around Him. Jesus trained the disciples before sending them to preach (See Mark 3:14). After Jesus, the early fathers of the New Testament Church also invested in others. This means that the subsequent generation failed to talk more about Jesus. Do you talk about Jesus? Let's talk more about Jesus. Let's talk more of His love.

Hospitability may also be a good consideration when it comes to evangelism. Today, hospitability may be a great challenge for the Christian. But the Christian should know that it is more noble to give than to receive from others. While serving the Lord, we are also advised to share what we have with others. Jesus spoke in parable to His disciples: "The King will reply, 'Truly I tell you, whatever you did for one of the least of these brothers and sisters of mine, you did for me.' (Matthew 25:40).

Can we forget prayer? The answer is no. Prayer is necessary in the life of the Christian. It is also necessary when we decide to do the work of evangelism. First, we must pray for the Holy Spirit to lead us in our walk with God. Apostle Paul said to the Corinthians that "A great door has been opened for me but there are adversaries" (1 Corinthians 16:9). John 10:10 makes us understand that the devil's mission is "to steal, to kill and to destroy." Ephesians 6:10 adds, "We are not fighting against flesh and blood but against principalities, rulers of darkness." For this reason, prayer is our weapon. Second, we must pray that God will open the eyes of our hearers so that after we have preached the Gospel and the Holy Spirit has convicted them of their sins, they wouldn't hesitate to give their lives to Christ. Third, we should pray continuously for all those we've ever preached to, that Christ will save them.

Follow-up is a great tool for soul-winning. After souls have come to Christ, it's our legitimate duty as Christians to pay frequent visit to the newly converts. We can also make phone calls or send text messages to inquire of their health, and pray for or with them; and also arrange to take them to church services whenever they are in need of help.

The Christian Disciple should bear in mind that, witnessing for Christ is never going to be an easy task. There is going to be opposition, turmoil, and even, in some cases, persuasion. Thus, we should not be surprised when we face challenges. But when they come, we should think about death to self, about the cross, about losing everything for the sake of the Gospel. Consider the story of Stephen (Acts 7:54–60).

In spite of dangers involved in discipleship, the instruction says, "Go therefore and make disciples" (Matthew 28:18–20). Jesus taught His disciples. And today, our first work as disciples is to bring people to the mercy of Christ and leave the judging of hearts to Him. Also, our mission of discipleship involves mission to the poor, the sick and the suffering, the imprisoned, and the psychopathic. The ultimate manifestation of discipleship is revealed in how we treat those around us who are in need.

The Christian is vigorously warned against rash judgements like who is a good Christian and a bad Christian, or whose name is in or out of the book of life. Certainly, we know that those who don't do God's will shall not enter into the Kingdom of God. Yet it is not my business to know who is in or out. Loving God and loving my neighbour should be my concern, and when Christ comes, He will let those who are ready in.

The end of the matter of discipleship is to show compassion and forgiveness and love. When Jesus was on earth, He displayed compassion. Besides compassion, He also showed forgiveness. Time and again, the disciples observed Jesus forgive the sins of many people. Our God is a compassionate God, and one result of that compassion was that He chose to save us from our sins, to forgive what otherwise would have led to our eternal loss. We are advised, as disciples, to emulate that trait of the character of God.

Second, Jesus openly associated with, taught, and advocated for the marginalised in His society. In the Gospel, Jesus sought to reach the upper classes as well, but at the same time, He ministered to the Gentiles, disputable women, the blind, lepers, publicans, demonised, Romans, those with disabilities, the poor, and a whole host of those considered outcasts, marginalised in one way or another from society. In addition, diversity and forms of discrimination were broken down by the Lord Jesus. The point is that Christ's death on the cross was for every human being. Moreover, it should remove all sense of bigotry towards any group of people.

"In Christ, ethnicities and social differences cease to be obstacles. God does not obliterate all ethnic differences in Christ, He redefines them, He enriches them, He reshapes them" (says John Piper, a founder and teacher of desiringGod.org and chancellor of Bethlehem College & Seminary).

All that we need to do is to follow the plan of Master Jesus concerning the Great Commission, to win more souls for Him. Evangelism is the heartbeat of God. God says to "go and make disciples" for Him. Just obey! Sharing the Gospel and teaching others whatever Christ commands us to do is an act of obedience to God and His word. As you have read to go and preach the Gospel, do not hesitate! Go! Go! Go!

7
The Cynosure of the Gospel
(The Gospel Is about Jesus)

THE WORD "CYNOSURE," pronounced "sainasuar" or "sina-suar," is prevalently used in American parlance and means a strong centre of interest and attraction. It can also mean an issue that is of a paramount importance that is hailed by all. Such a notion is always at the pinnacle of affairs and has no parallels whatsoever. In this chapter of our discovery and truth, the Gospel puts Jesus at the zenith of affairs. We can therefore hold the uppermost idea that the locus of the Gospel is Jesus.

The word "gospel" means, basically, good news. It is the good news that Christ has instituted for humanity what we could ever do for ourselves. It means that the penalty for our sins has been fully paid by the Lord Jesus Christ. God will forgive us anything that we have ever done wrong no matter our past wrongdoings and sins. One interesting thing about the Gospel is that the perfect life of Jesus is now credited to us, as if we ourselves lived as sinlessly as did Christ. It means that we can now be connected with the Lord Jesus Christ, who will give us the power to live a life of faith and obedience. What is more, the gospel means that we are no longer cut off from God and alienated from His eternal kingdom. To conclude, we can boldly say that we are now children of God, and this is because we are now part of His heavenly family.

Diversity in meanings of the Gospel of Christ makes every Christian so happy and gives us hope that, if we change our present lifestyles and follow the statutes, precepts, and commandments of God, we are already winners; we can stand the chance of eternal salvation. What a good news, and this is all about the Gospel. To make all this possible, the centrality is through Jesus Christ. Who is Jesus then?

Many a person sends messages through our cell phones telling humanity who Jesus is. In the subject of chemistry, these people claim that "He turned water into wine" (John 2:6–10). In biology, Jesus was born without the normal conception (Isaiah 7:14; Luke 1:26–27). In physics, He disproved the law of gravity when He ascended into the heavens (Acts 1:11). In economics, Jesus disproved the law of diminishing return by feeding five thousand men with just two fish and five loaves of bread (Matthew 14:19, 6:13). In the medical field, Jesus cured the sick, the blind, and so on without administration of a single dose of drugs (Matthew 8:2–4; Mark 1:29–31; Luke 11:4; John 4:46–54).Jesus is the beginning and the end, the Alpha and Omega (Revelation 22:13, 21:6; John 1:1–15). He fills the elements of history. It is also said that "He shall be called Wonderful, Counsellor, Mighty God, Prince of Peace"—what a perfect government! (Isaiah 9:6–7). Perhaps the ultimate of what Jesus is in religious matters— "No one comes to the Father except through Me" (See John 14:4–6). Without Jesus, Christianity ceases to exist, because the Gospel about Christianity is all about Jesus—His birth, His ministry (His teachings, His prayer life, His healings, His miracles), His death and resurrection, and His second coming.

Indeed, Jesus is the greatest Man in history. That's why the centre of the Gospel is all about Him. Our concern in this biblical study is about His birth, His ministry, His crucifixion, His death, His resurrection, and His second coming.

When Jesus commanded His disciples to preach the Gospel, He was indeed certain about His life and ministry. The disciples were to talk about His birth, which the scientific and synthetic world do not accept. Jesus was God and is God who came in human form and was born of a woman, who was a sinner. Jesus was a God born in a manger, though He claimed Himself to be the King of kings. These assertions do not make sense to the ordinary.

Over the centuries, there has been much debate about the true identity of Jesus. Some argued strongly that He was John the Baptist. There were others who said that Jesus was Elijah or Jeremiah or even one of the prophets. Controversy galore! However, in spite of scientific applications to Bible teachings, faith in Jesus as the Saviour of the world now prevails.

For all of us, our existence began when we were born. Jesus was different—He did not come into existence in Mary's womb. He was there before the earth was created. That is what we mean by pre-existence. He was there before all time. Isaiah 9:6 teaches us about the eternal pre-existence of Jesus, considered a special Person Who was to come into the world. It is an extraordinary claim that this One (Jesus) would be called, among other titles, "Mighty God" and "Everlasting Father." Other Bible writers show that Jesus existed before the world began, before He was conceived as a man. Luke 19:10 gives testimony to this fact: "The Son of Man, came to seek and to save what was lost." Jesus acknowledged His own pre-existence with the Father before He came to earth. Jesus spoke of His own existence with the Father before coming to save humanity and remained in constant communion with God while here on earth. An explicit statement from Jesus came in the words of His great passion week prayer when He asked His Father to glorify Him, "with the glory I had with you before the world began" (John 17:5). In addition, He said, "Before Abraham was, I am" (John 8:58).

Four major biblical testimonies illustrate Jesus's deity: John 1:1–3, 14; Matthew 1:21–23; Galatians 4:4; and Hebrews 1:8. In this illustration, God says of the Son, "Your throne, O God, will last for ever and ever" (Hebrews 1:8). God the Father introduces the Son as God at His incarnation.

"In the beginning was the Word, and the Word was with God, and the Word was God. He was with God in the beginning. Through Him all things were made, without Him nothing was made that has been made." (John 1:1–3)

"She will give birth to a son, and you are to give him the name Jesus, because he will save his people from their sins. All this took place to fulfil what the Lord had said through the prophet: "The virgin will be a child and will give birth to a son, and they will call him Immanuel—which means, God with us."" (Matthew 1:21–23)

"But when the time had fully come, God sent his Son, born of a woman, born under law, that we might receive the full rights of the Son." (Galatians 4:4)

At the very tender age of twelve, Jesus started His ministry. Once, Jesus told His earthly parents (Mary and Joseph) the need for Him to do the will of His Father. According to Jesus, the Father's work is to preach to sinners, to tell sinners about eternal life and the Kingdom of God. The Sermon on the Mount of Olives (Matthew 5–7) stands as the most significant sermon ever preached, Jesus presented not an impossible idealism or a perfectionist legalism but a standard of conduct for those saved by His grace. Here, Jesus taught about humility, grace, and faith. Besides, Jesus taught humanity how to pray and also how to address God "Our Father in heaven. Hallowed be your name" anytime we pray.

The works of Jesus at this time made it evident that He was truly the Messiah. He did not come simply to speak of a future hope; He showed that God's kingdom is filled with love and compassion free from sin and suffering. This could become a reality for every disciple of Christ Jesus.

Jesus, fresh from the Sermon on the Mount, confronted a leper and healed him. He calmed the storm and had power over demons. He healed the paralytic and a woman with a haemorrhage. In addition, He brought Jarius's daughter back to life. In a way, Jesus had power over nature. His disciples were amazed. "What kind of man is this? Even the winds and the waves obey Him" (Matthew 8:27). This was a statement made by His disciples. Despite the good deeds done by Jesus, He had a lot of enemies who decided to crucify Him. Jesus's whole purpose in coming to earth was to die for humankind. No matter how good His life was, the end result would inevitably be death. It had to be that way for the plan of salvation to be implemented. The consistent note through the Gospel is that Jesus was born to die. His death was not accident. It had to happen.

The story of the Resurrection of Jesus is told in Matthew 27:62–66 and 28:1–15. Several events may be pivotal to Christianity, among them the Incarnation, His suffering, the cross, His death, and His second coming. But in a sense, the Resurrection triumph them all. Without the Resurrection, nothing else matters. Resurrection is the central doctrine of the Christian faith.

Of all the world religions, Judaism and Christianity are the only two that espouse the concept of a resurrection as such. Read Matthew 28 for details and the significance of the Resurrection of Jesus. During the Resurrection, many people were brought back to life. These individuals were seen by friends and loved ones, who also gave testimony of the risen Saviour. Because of the Resurrection of Jesus, we too have the hope of resurrection. Otherwise death is the final end of us all—including Christians. As a Christian, always bear in mind that, without resurrection, the plan of salvation would be in vain. Thus, Jesus's resurrection is our hope.

In short, the Resurrection of Jesus was an actual event witnessed by many people, including the disciples. The following passages from Bible can help Christians crystallise their hopes in the Resurrection of Jesus.

- John 5:25–29
  "I tell you the truth, a time is coming and has come when the dead will hear the voice of the son of God and those who hear will live. For as the Father has life in himself, so he has granted the Son to have life in himself. And he has given him authority to judge because he is the Son of Man. Do not be amazed at this, for a time is coming when all who are in their graves will hear his voice and come out— those who have done good will rise to live, and those who have done evil will rise to be condemned."
- John 11:23–26
  Jesus said to her, "Your brother will rise again." Martha answered, "I know he will rise again in the resurrection at the last day. Jesus said to her, "I am the resurrection and the life. He who believes in me will live, even though he dies; and whoever lives and believes in me will never die. Do you believe this?"
- 1 Corinthians 15:51–58
  "Listen, I tell you a mystery. We will not all asleep, but we will be changed—in a flesh, in the twinkling of an eye, at the last trumpet. For the trumpet will sound, the dead will be raised imperishable, and we will be changed. For the perishable must clothe itself with the imperishable, and the mortal with immortality. When the perishable, and the mortal with immortality, then the saying that is written will come true: "Death has been swallowed up in victory."

  "Where, O death, is your victory? Where, O death, is your sting?"

  The sting of death is sin, and the power of sin is law. But thanks be to God! He has given us the victory through our Lord Jesus Christ. Therefore, my dear brothers, stand firm. Let nothing move you. Always give yourselves fully to the work of the Lord, because you know that your labour in the Lord is not in vain."

- 1 Thessalonians 4:13–18

  "Brothers, we do not want you to be ignorant about those who fall asleep, or to grieve like the rest of men, who have no hope. We believe that Jesus died and rose again and so we believe that God will bring with Jesus those who have fallen asleep in him. According to the Lord's own word, we tell you that we who are still alive, who are left till the coming of the Lord, will certainly not precede those who have fallen asleep. For the Lord himself will come down from heaven, with a loud command, with the voice of the archangel and with the trumpet call of God, and the dead in Christ will rise first. After that, we who are still alive and are left will be caught up together with them in the clouds to meet the Lord in the air. And so we will be with the Lord for ever. Therefore, encourage each other with these words."

The above scriptural text guarantee our own resurrection. We should therefore cling to the doctrines of Christ for our mutual benefit. It is prudent to note that Jesus, who has risen and gone to the Father (God), will come a second time. This is the evidence in the text below.

"So Christ was sacrificed once to take away the sins of many people; and he will appear a second time, not to bear sin, but to bring salvation to those who are waiting for him." (Hebrews 9:28)

The promise of Christ's return is sure. Christ gave the disciples many signs of His second coming. Those signs of His coming were not designed to bring about fear in the hearts of the disciples but to show them what to expect and how to know when His coming was near. The Lord Jesus has given us many signs. Read Matthew 24 for more details. As we see, and have already read and seen, the fulfilment of these things, we know and hope that His coming is near.

There are those who torture and abuse others, those who murder and exploit, who plunder and pillage, and who rob the coffers of their governments, leaving millions to suffer in degradation and poverty. And there are good people who arrogantly turn their backs on God and His gracious offer of mercy and pardon. It would be the height of irresponsibility and a great mistake to give them the impression that the Second Coming holds anything for them but bad news, unless they change and come to Christ. With people's eternal destiny depending on these issues, it would be criminal on our part to sugarcoat the reality of the situation. If you are in the category of these people, the essential thing at the moment is that you should repent. Read Philippians 2:12 to alert yourself.

The Gospel is found only in God's word; and no messenger of God talks about Jesus and the gospel without referring to the Bible. Any preacher or Bible teacher who does such is not from God. True men of God do not contradict the Bible.

The Gospel is not for business. To many people, the gospel is for business. Many calling themselves men of God are serving money and pleasures of this earth not God. Others are selling prophecies, anointing oil, prayers, healings, and miracles for money. Read Luke 16:13–15 and Acts 8:18–21 for more details. Today, most people stop working and schooling for bizarre reasons, and enter into the pastoral ministry, which is bad! Let the Christian live a life free from covetousness.

In conclusion, let God's children understand that the Gospel is all about Jesus Christ of Nazareth. Let's now begin to talk more about Jesus. Moreover, while preaching about the Gospel of Christ, let us also live as Christ lived—His goodness, kindness, gentleness, faithfulness, genuineness, and love for everyone.

8
The Essentiality of Jesus
(The Need for Jesus in Your Life)

ANYTHING THAT IS described as essential in any language is of paramount importance. Such a thing could be described as salient, important, vital, or significant. Water, food, and air are essential elements for the survival of living things. Without these elements, life would be impossible.

During creation, for example, the Creator saw the essential things needed by a particular creature before the creation of such a creature. Consider the creation of beasts and their kinds and everything that creeps on the earth. God found that land was essential to these creatures. Hence, He made dry land available. Even before God created the first human being, He had already prepared for him ground, land, water, green vegetation, light, fruits, and so on. What was crucial at this stage during creation was God saw that it was essential for His representative on earth to have dominion over His creatures. So God created humanity in His own image (Genesis 1:27).

What is more is that God blessed them and said to them, "Be fruitful and multiply...and have dominion over every living thing that moves on the earth" (verse 28). Getting someone to have dominion over living things on earth was very essential to God. The creation of a male and a female was of paramount importance to God. Without the union of a male and a female, how are they going to "be fruitful and multiply" (verse 28)? Thus God created Eve from the rib of Adam (man). Eve was to become a companion of Adam. Eve became Adam's second self, showing the close union and affectionate attachment that should exist in this relation. "For no man ever yet hated his own flesh; but nourishes and cherishes it." (Ephesians 5:29)

When God created humankind, He freely gave freedom to them to make their choices. God desires from all His creatures the service of love—service that springs from an appreciation of His character. God's essential thing recommended at this stage is a deep sense of love. God's love became supreme, and love for one another gained popularity. There was no note of discord to mar the celestial harmonies.

After the creation of Adam, every living creature was brought before him to receive its name. Adam saw that to each had been given a companion, but among them, there was not found a helper meant for him. And God said, "It is not good for the man to be alone; I will make him a helper suitable for him." Humans were not made to dwell alone. As a result of Adam's solitary situation, Eve was created. She was to be the companion of Adam. God placed the couple in the eastern part of the Garden of Eden. Eden bloomed on earth. Adam and Eve had free access to long life. There were no signs of sin. "The morning stars sang together and all the angels shouted for joy" (Job 38:7). What was significant to God was perfect peace and joy.

God placed humanity under law—an indispensable element of every governmental structure. God told the first human beings to eat from every tree that had the characteristics of yielding seed. They were to use them as food, including every beast of the earth, every bird of the sky, and everything that moved on the earth that had life in it. In addition, God gave every green plant to humankind as a supplement to their food needs. What is so amazing is that some of these plants have medicinal value for humankind—ginger may help relieve headaches and joint pain; garlic is antibacterial and antiviral, and it helps boost your immune function. The Bible says, "God saw all that He had made, and it was very good." (Genesis 1:31)

All the trees shared the common characteristics of being "pleasing to the sight and good for food." Though pleasing to look at and good for food, one of the trees was not good for humanity. Eating its fruits would give the partaker a knowledge of good and evil and would certainly produce death. God did not hide the consequences of eating from the forbidden tree to the couple. God declared, "You are free to eat from any tree in the garden, but you must not eat from the tree of the knowledge of good and evil, for when you eat from it, you will certainly die" (Genesis 2:16–17). God's manifestation of deeper love is demonstrated to our first parents.

As long as Adam and Eve remained loyal to the divine law, their capacity to know, to enjoy, and to love would continually increase. Unfortunately, this couple became disloyal to God due to the seductive words and lies given to this couple. Sin entered the world full of God's glory. Disobedience! Despite several warnings given to our early parents, Satan used his wiles to outsmart the couple to sin against God. As Satan used the serpent as his medium, our parents transgressed the command of God. Their sin brought guilt and sorrow upon the world, and had it not been for the goodness and mercy of God, it would have plunged the race into hopelessness. What would be the consequences of this transgression?

"The wages of sin is death" (Romans 6:23) should be the answer. The law of God cannot be transgressed with impunity, so sentence was pronounced upon the father of humankind. After their sin, Adam and Eve were no longer to dwell in Eden. Eden means the presence of God. Our first parents felt sorry for the offence they had committed against their Maker. Humankind's disobedience is the cause of all the troubles and pains in our world. Our first parents realised later they were naked. God's love would not cease to be extended to humankind.

When God saw that Adam and his wife had transgressed His law and that the couple was naked, He clothed them with the skin of an animal. At the killing of an animal, blood was spilled, symbolising the Crucifixion of Jesus. What a compassion manifested by God! The enormity of God's love is not at its climax. We, as human beings, should be thankful to God for giving us His Son Jesus to die for our sins. With Jesus, humanity has hope, big with immortality.

We need Jesus as a compass to life. This is because He is a guide to success and everything in life. Jesus died for us, and He is our Saviour. When humanity sinned, Christ decided to come to earth to save humanity from damnation. Jesus offers light and salvation to sinful people. The name Jesus even charms our fears. It is life, health, and peace.

In scripture, Jesus delighted to speak of God as the Father. According to the four Gospels (Matthew, Mark, Luke, and John), Jesus applied the name Father to God. On various occasions, He added the following qualifiers: "Heavenly Father" (Matthew 6:14), "living Father" (John 6:57), "Holy Father" (John 17:11), and "righteous Father" (John 17:25). The name describes the intimate bond that should unite us to God (the Father). This illustrates the fact that Jesus is a link between us sinners and God, Who alone has the power to forgive us all our sins. Why then do you choose to ignore Jesus in your life? Jesus came to the earth to reveal God to humanity. According to Jesus, as human beings, sinners of course, we have a loving Father Who is concerned with the needs of His children. God, our Father, is in heaven, Who is a caring Father. This truth is only revealed to humanity through Jesus.

In some different ways, Jesus taught and demonstrated that three Divine Persons constitute the Godhead, and they are God the Father, God the Son, and God the Holy Spirit. When Jesus's earthly ministry was about to end, He promised His disciples that He would send the Holy Spirit, the Comforter. Here again, we see the three Persons working together. "I will pray to the Father," Jesus assured them, "and

He will give you another Helper, that He may abide with you forever... the Spirit of truth." (John 14:16–17 NKJV)

Jesus explained that there is a complete harmony and cooperation among the three Divine Persons in the plan of salvation. As the Son glorified the Father, demonstrating His love, so the Holy Spirit glorifies the Son, revealing His grace and love to the world as well.

Jesus (the Son) came to emphasise that the Father looks at us with incomparable love (See Jeremiah 31:3). "Behold what manner of love the Father has bestowed on us, that we should be called children of God" (1 John 3:1 NKJV). It is amazing that the Almighty God, Who rules the immense universe, would allow us insignificant and poor sinners living on a tiny planet in the midst of so many galaxies to call Him Father. He does so because He loves us. Even long before Jesus was nailed on the cross, our Father (God) had already loved us, before the foundation of the earth. Rely on Jesus for your salvation.

While Jesus is described in the scriptures as the truth (John 14:6), God's truth is revealed in a supreme way in the Person of Jesus Christ. A true knowledge of God is given to us in Jesus of Whom the Bible speaks, because God has revealed Himself through Him.

In John 16:13, we are told that the Spirit of truth will guide us into all truth. He does this by pointing to Christ and by helping us remember what has been said and done for us.

The life of Jesus teaches us to be responsible beings on earth. The broken heart is touched upon your rendezvous with Him. In addition, He is healed upon a personal contact with Jesus. Jesus changed the life of Zacchaeus, but Judas refused to change. To become a new person, just go to Master Jesus for transformation. He is ever ready to change you.

Last, Jesus promises humanity eternal life. Because of our sins, we deserve to die. But Christ took our place on the cross and paid the death penalty that otherwise rested on us. Being innocent, Jesus took on our guilt and received our punishment so that we, being sinful, could be declared innocent. Through Christ, instead of perishing we receive eternal life. John 3:15 makes this amazing promise to us. It says, "Whoever believes in Him should not perish but have eternal life," a promise repeated at the end of John 3:16.

When Jesus becomes our Saviour, our life acquires a whole new meaning, and we can enjoy a richer and fuller existence. Jesus said, "I have come that they may have life, and have it to the full" (John 10:10b).

During His earthly ministry, Jesus asked His disciples, "Who do people say the Son of Man is?" (Matthew 16:13). Difficult question indeed. The next riddle Jesus put across was, "But what about you?" "Who do you say I am?" Answers to the two questions were given by Jesus Himself. But first, Peter, by faith, gave the response, "You are the Messiah, the Son of the living God" (Matthew 16:16). This title, "the Son of Man," was Jesus's favourite title expressed by Himself.

Scriptures present Jesus as a true human being. He was born as a baby, grew up as a child, and did everything as an ordinary human being would do. Unfortunately, many failed to recognise that there is more to be found in this title. Many people worshipped Him. These included the disciples on the sea (Matthew 14:33), the healing of the blind man (John 9:38), and the women at the tomb of Jesus (Matthew 28:9). All worshipped Jesus openly, recognising His deity. Jesus was aware of God's commandments that say, "You shall have no other gods before me," "You shall not make for yourself an image in the form of anything in heaven above or on the earth beneath or in the waters below," and "You shall not bow down to them or worship them" (Exodus 20:3–5). But when the people worshipped Him, He did not stop them because He is God.

The Key Teachings of Jesus.

This edition of our endeavour in the treatment of *Fragments* is essentially designed to suit the key teachings of Jesus. Anything described as being the "key" is epitome of it—the best possible example of that particular thing. In this instance, for example, an attempt is made to look at the best teachings of our Lord Jesus Christ.

Enough has been said about Jesus—His birth, baptism, deity, you name it. In the New Testament, for example, Jesus is presented as both human and divine. Jesus's two natures, human and divine, are inseparable. In John 1:1, the scriptures declare that the Word Who is God, the same God "became flesh and made His dwelling among us" (verse 14). This explains the fact that Jesus is both God and man. In Christian theology, this is referred to as "Hypostatic Union." What is so amazing about Jesus is that at the time of His existence on the earth, He was described as a teacher. The Jews referred to Jesus as Rabbi, meaning Teacher.

His contemporaries acknowledged Him as a Teacher, for He exhibited the general characteristics of any teacher during His time. As was the practice, He would sit down to teach. Sometimes, He quoted the scriptures and then commented on them. Last, Jesus had a group of disciples who attentively listened to Him and followed and served. In fact, Jesus was the greatest mentor during His time.

Fundamental differences between Jesus and the other religious teachers, however, did exist. While other teachers concentrated mostly on the intellectual aspects of a subject, Jesus addressed the whole being of His audience. As a result, those who heard Jesus "were amazed at His teaching, for He taught them as one having authority, and not as the teachers of the law" (Mark 1:22). Great authority accompanied the ministry of Jesus. He rebuked demons (See Luke 4:35–36); He cured sicknesses (See Luke 4:39–40), and raised the dead (See Luke11:38–44; Mark 5:21–43). One important thing Jesus did in His teachings is the theme of truth. Jesus taught because He is "the truth."

One condition for receiving the gift of the Holy Spirit is repentance. Jesus promised to send the Holy Spirit as His representative on condition that we repent and have faith in Him. Any double-minded person cannot expect to receive anything from God. We should repent and believe that God is able to do all our wishes according to

His will. This promise is expressed in Matthew 3:2, "Repent, for the Kingdom of God has come near."

Repentance is not simple conviction of sin. Thus the feeling of guilt and shame for sin because one has been found out. It is also not trying to be religious. And it is not also being sorry for a wrong-doing. Repentance is the complete change of heart and mind. It is a godly grief for sin; and it involves the new way we think about sin. This makes us turn from sin. This change of mind involves the intellect. The change of heart involves our emotions and will. Judas changed his mind and not his will (Source: Bible Study Outline 2004, The Church of Pentecost, complied by Apostle Dr. Alfred Koduah).

Jesus presented His teachings to different audiences, being careful to adapt His method to each person. Sometimes, He preached a congregational sermon; other times, He dialogued with individuals or groups. At one point in time, He taught openly; other times He left His disciples in suspense. Also, during His teachings, He would approach individuals as well as His opponents, showing His nature of forgiveness.

What is important about Christ's teachings is that He teaches about God and things pertaining to spiritual and practical lives. Moreover, Jesus was an example of what He taught—He was loving, gentle, meek, patient, self-controlled, faithful, and peaceful. Jesus was not hateful, violent, punitive, torturing, vindictive, and rude. If this was how He lived, then we must follow and worship Him.

Other things Jesus taught include we should get ourselves prepared as though we were children, we should not commit murder, and as humans, we should live peacefully with our neighbours. In addition, Jesus taught that our choices should be based on His will, and this in consequence will lead us into eternal salvation. Love for one another should be a yardstick to hold by any Christian. This means that love goes beyond religion, ethnocentrism, or tribalism.

In one of His teachings, He discussed adultery. Jesus said: "You have heard that it was said, 'You shall not commit adultery.' But I tell you that anyone who looks at a woman lustfully has already committed adultery with her in his heart" (Matthew 5:27–28). In all His teachings, it is acknowledged that Christ wants us to love ourselves and live as a family.

On another occasion, Jesus teaches about peace and prays for peace. He says, "Peace I leave with you; my peace I give you. I do not give to you as the world gives. Do not let your hearts be troubled and do not be afraid" (John 14:27).

To crown it all, Jesus came on a mission to save humanity from eternal damnation. He taught us, in the Great Commission, to "go and make disciples" (Matthew 28:18–20). This means that we have received God's messages free of charge; we did not pay for it. Likewise, we as Christians should also go and spread the Gospel through all abroad so that countries of people who are cut off from this message will also receive God's message. In the end, they will be saved. In addition, while we go out to spread the Gospel, there is only one name that we know, and that name is Jesus, Who is the Saviour of the world.

9
God's Judgement
(God's Judgement for Humanity)

GOD'S JUDGEMENT DAY in a biblical sense is the last day of the world, when all people will be judged by God for what they have done while living on earth. Besides the Christian doctrine, other religious hold a similar view of one day when God will reward people according to their deeds but punish the wicked and condemn them into an eternal lake of fire.

Christian history is full of dark pages. Horrible things have been done by professed followers of Christ, and according to our understanding of Bible prophecy, more evil things will be done in God's name before Jesus returns. When Jesus returns in His second coming, He is going to judge the faithful and the unfaithful. The question is, "Why do you look at the speck of sawdust in your brother's eye and pay no attention to the plank in your own eye?" (Matthew 7:3). Human beings don't make that judgement. Judgement of this nature is the prerogative of God.

Before the final reward is given, it must be decided which born-again Christians are fit to share the inheritance of the righteous. Christ is going to reward the faithful. His reward is with Him "to give every man according as His work shall be" (Revelation 22:12). When Jesus comes again, we will put on the glorious, new immortal body that He will provide for His redeemed. Who will constitute the redeemed?

From the constant reaching and perspective of the Bible reading, it is observed that even though the Christian who stands at the judgement seat of Christ will suffer loss, they may be saved. This should not encourage any Christian to refrain from living righteous life.

At the Second Coming of Christ, the promise is to take His followers to where He has prepared (See John 14:1–3). Apostle Paul adds the detail that those followers include the living and those who will be resurrected from their graves (See 1 Thessalonians 4:16–17). John adds another detail: After the first resurrection at the Second Coming, the remainder of the dead will stay dead until the thousand years end (Revelation 20:5).

Before the final destruction of the wicked, the saved are given the chance to know more about their questions. Even more amazing, the redeemed play a role in judging the lost. The question for post-mortem examination in the light of God's judgement is, "Who are to be judged?"

Now, the Christian must not take the outcome of God's final judgement for granted. Let us pray to God to have mercy upon us while serving Him faithfully by doing whatever He tells us through His word. What can we do for those who have not believed in God's only Son Jesus? Christ tells us what we can do. In His sermon, He says, "Go and make disciples of all nations, baptising them in the name of the Father and of the Son and of the Holy Spirit" (Matthew 28:19). Here, Jesus tells us to go and tell sinners about the good news. The question is, "Are you ready to go?"

One of our great self-deception is to say, "Who sees us?" and think we can sin in the secret. For this reason, we steal, we lie, we kill, and do a whole lot of evil things, thinking that no one sees us—we forget that God is watching everyone. Jeremiah 23:24 says, "Who can hide in secret place so that I cannot see them?" declares the Lord. "Do not I fill heaven and earth" declares the Lord. The question now is, "If we human beings cannot hide from God, how can we hide our sins from Him?"

When it comes to judgement, I can't fathom why we Christians always judge people. We've even become a hindrance to sinners who would have come to worship God with us because we will judge their way of life—their dressing, their level of education, and so on. But we forget that, as humans, we all have flaws. Read Romans 3:23 to advice you.

Stop judging others! Judgement belongs to God. It was Jesus Himself who gave the command, "Judge not" (Matthew 7:1). Jesus wants us to be humble, kind, gentle, and good to others. Help those who are in need rather than judging them.

There are two separate judgements. Christians will be judged at the Judgement Seat of Christ (See Romans 14:10–12). This judgement does not determine our salvation. Apostle Paul said in 1 Corinthians 3:11–15 that we should be careful of the foundation we build upon because the Judgement Seat will reveal whether we built on gold, silver, and precious stones of good works in Christ, or what we built on the foundation may be the wood, hay, and stubble of worthless with no spiritual value. We will give an account for our actions, whether they reflected the life of a true Christian.

The second judgement is those who rejected Christ as their Saviour. Their thoughts, words, actions, and conscience will be judged against the perfect standard of God. Their punishment will be eternal condemnation to the hell fire (See 2 Peter 2:4).

In summer 2010 during Children's ministry programme of the Church of Pentecost in Italy, a presentation was made with the title "Leading Our Children to Christ." A lot of questions were asked by parents who attended the programme. First among those questions were, "Will all children inherit the Kingdom of heaven?" and "What does the Bible say about children under this condition?"

As Christians, we believe that anyone who dies without believing in Jesus as Lord and Saviour will not inherit the Kingdom of God, and they will miss heaven and finally face God's wrath (according to 1 Corinthians 6:9; Galatians 5:19–21; and Revelation 22:15). Making the matter worse, we are made to believe that all have sinned from birth (See Psalm 51:5). This obviously includes children.

However, children are incapable of fully understanding God's requirements for salvation. The question is, "Will God judge children even though they don't understand salvation?" Since children are considered innocent, it is easy to say that they will not face God's judgement (Read Deuteronomy 1:39).

Nonetheless, God instructs every parent to "Train up a child in a way he should go, and when he is old he will not depart from it" (Proverbs 22:6). It is required of the Christian to be faithful in everything God has entrusted in his or her care because every steward will render an account to God. As a parent, you are a steward of your children, and as a steward, it is your duty to raise your children in the fear of God and to teach them to be socially responsible. Also, training the youth to respect the elders among them is scriptural (See Ephesians 6:1).

The Role of Parents and Pastors.
Bible teachers and pastors, who are overseers of God's flock, are to cherish the flock. The Christian leader should teach and discipline in every area of the Christian moral life. Leaders are to intercede for the flock and ask for them God's strength and power to live a blameless life before God.

Conclusion.
We have an inheritance, incorruptible and undefiled, and it is laid up for us in heaven. Get ready for your inheritance! There are five crowns mentioned in the New Testament that will be given to the faithful Christian. They are the Incorruptible Crown (1 Corinthians 9:24–25), the Crown of Rejoicing (1 Thessalonians 2:19), the Crown of Righteous (2 Timothy 4:8), the Crown of Glory (1 Peter 5:4), and the

Crown of Life (Revelation 2:10). Before we get to heaven for this glorious inheritance, we need to prove ourselves worthy of emulation to receive the inheritance. Therefore, as Christians, we need to eschew ourselves from anything that hinders us from doing the will of God.

10
Heaven as a Promise
(Someone's Dream)

THERE IS ONE Italian living in a county called *Schio* in the province of *Vicenza*, Italy. Much as he remains pious, he is born into a Catholic family. Dario, as he is called, has a firm belief in the existence of God. He also believes God created the Universe. Though Dario is religious, he is not a Christian. He knows about God but lacks faith in Him. This is the vast difference between knowing God and knowing about God.

Notwithstanding Dario's lack of faith in God, this gentleman is an intelligent personality exhibiting the character of a gentle soul. What's more is that Dario possesses the spirit of loving and is always kind to everyone. To Dario, Heaven is a myth.

It is believed that there may be countless of Darios the whole world over. It must be noted that whether you argue like Dario, heaven is not a myth. Heaven should not be taken for fancy. Heaven is real. If one doubts the reality of this place, consider the biblical message of Jesus recorded in the Gospel according to Matthew 6:9–10: "This, then, is how you should pray: 'Our Father in heaven, hallowed be your name, your kingdom come, your will be done on earth as it is in heaven.'"

From the scriptural text above, we can see that God lives in heaven, and therefore, heaven is real. Despite numerous appeals to Dario during our Bible studies encounter, he would always prove to be recalcitrant, pushing away the notion that heaven is real. There's an adage that says, "You can lead a horse to water but you can't make it drink." So we left Dario for God to "deal" with him.

When the right time came, God opened the mind's door of this unbeliever. And now, Dario is a born-again Christian. How did this all important repentance happen?

"Sam, he said: In my dream, I found myself lying on my bed. Suddenly, I stepped out of my body, and then was lifted up through the roof of my house and my whole life just passed before my eyes in just an instant. Then the cloud opened up and I saw multitudes of people in a long queue. Everyone was nervous to know what was going on.

Then we saw angels. The angels had no physical bodies like humans. There was radiating dazzling light wherever they went. They were more than giants. They were neither male nor female. I can't describe them to the height of any human being. They had wings. Then I asked myself, 'How does God look compared to these beautiful and powerful creatures?'"

He continued, "Sam, It takes nanoseconds to move from one place to another. It was magical. Heaven is so beautiful. There is no place on earth like heaven. Then we heard the angels singing. Initially, we didn't understand the song until one of the angels said, 'My Lord, give them ears to understand our language.' Then I realised that heaven has its language. The song said,

> 'You are worthy, Lord.
> You are worthy, Lord.
> We give You praise.
> You are worthy, Lord.
> Ancient of Days,
> You are worthy, Lord.
> We give You praise.
> You are worthy, Lord.'"

"Getting closer to the throne of God, we saw someone who sat on a big throne. We couldn't see His face because the place was brighter than the daylight. We heard the angels talking to the One Who sat on the throne; and when He speaks, the angels would respond, 'Yes, my Lord and King!'"

"Sam, in less than thirty minutes, we were taken to a different place, it was like standing on a hill, and we were given the chance to see all the peoples on earth. We were so excited! I saw multitudes of people, both great and small. I could see everything people were doing on earth. I saw those who called themselves Christians: A pastor who was stealing money from the church coffers, and some Christians who were passionately involved in sin, and those who were killing the innocent, and those who were begging for food, and no one gave them. Again, I saw those who were practising abortion, and those who were causing divisions in the body of Christ, and some politicians who were drinking blood. Then I began to cry."

"Sam, I heard the voice of the One Who sat on the throne. He said to me that if I was satisfied with my life on earth and I told him no. Then He said he was going to show me hell. Hell was a horrible place. Yet there were millions of people living in hell. You can't ever get out. It was like a volcano. He showed me a horrible man who was mean and prideful. This man's friends and loved ones showed him that he needed to find Christ. But the man said "I don't need to find God. We are all Gods." "He had no compassion for anyone before his death. Now he is reaping the consequences of his actions," said the One Who sat on the throne."

"Again, He showed me another horrible man who was very mean to his wife when he was alive. He said to me that this man's wife was like a slave to him. He maltreated his wife and even stopped her from worshipping God and doing good to others. This man's friends advised him to be kind and loving to his wife but he wouldn't listen. To this man too, the One Who sat on the throne said to me that he is reaping the consequences of his actions, and it is too late for him to repent."

"Finally, He asked me: "Are you sorry for your sins? I said: "Yes, I am." Then an angel said to us that it was time for us to go back to earth. I heard the One Who sat on the throne, "Go back and worship me in spirit and in truth." In a twinkle of an eye, we found ourselves on earth; and I woke up from my sleep, only to see that I was dreaming. 'Oh my God! Was this a dream?' I shouted! And this is my testimony, said Dario"

Heaven is the dwelling place of God. The Bible says, "In the beginning God created the heavens and earth." (Genesis 1:1). The bottom line is that heaven exists.

The Bible describes heaven as the "New Jerusalem." The streets are constructed with pure gold, like transparent glass. There would be no need for a sun or moon, and no need for earthly buildings, and no need for money, and no need for electricity. We will live in a place where things are different from our world. In heaven, the presence of God will be its light. There is a tree of life in heaven (Revelation 22:2). Heaven is not a place for human beings. That's why God will first translate our earthly bodies, and we will have new bodies (1 Corinthians 15:51–58). We will be with the angels of God. In heaven, there will be no tears, no pain, and no sorrow (Revelation 21:4).

Do you want to go to this place—heaven? If yes, give your life to Jesus. Let Jesus be the Lord and Saviour of your life. When you do that, He will lead you to heaven because He is the only way to God, our Father, Who art in heaven.

The truth is that not all of us would have this supernatural encounter with God, about heaven and hell. It is believed that some of us will have this experience while others will not. There are a lot of people who claim to have gone to heaven, hell, the spirit realm, and so on. Whether they are true or not, we don't know. Human beings don't make that judgement. It is only God Who can tell. Notwithstanding the situation, God, heaven, and hell still exist as said the Bible. What's more important is that we rely on God to know the truth, because He has given us Jesus, Who is the Truth. By obeying God's Word and being faithful to Him, Christ will take us to heaven, His dwelling place as promised in John 14:2.

Heaven is real!

11
God Cares for You
(God Has Plans for You)

WE SAY: "NOBODY cares about me!" People felt the same in Bible Times (Deuteronomy 28:54; 2 Samuel 19:6). In John 5:7, the invalid replied to Jesus, "I have no one to help me into the pool when the water is stirred. While I am trying to get in, someone goes down ahead of me." He felt being rejected by his neighbours. Ignominy, He didn't know that God had good plans for him. This incidence occurs daily in our lives—at times, we feel God has abandoned us and no one cares for us. I really learned this the hard way—I felt God had abandoned me—I now believe that God cares for me and also has good plans for my future. So I always rely on God and not man.

In this chapter, the main focus is to introduce you to a God Who cares for you. He also has good plans for your future. Jeremiah 29:11 says, "For I know the plans I have for you." Declares the Lord, "plans to prosper you and not to harm you, plans to give you hope and a future."

Truthfully, life can be purposeless. Sometimes, we wonder why bad things happen to good people and why good things happen to bad people. We scream that "Life is not fair!" It makes sense for a drug dealer to be in prison. It makes sense for a reckless driver to be in a serious accident. It makes sense for a prostitute to acquire HIV and AIDS. But what about the innocent child who is diagnosed with HIV? What about the innocent man who is killed by a terrorist and leaves his family behind? What about the preacher who is sent to prison for preaching the Gospel? What about the faithful Christian who seeks for children and doesn't have them. If I were to continue with numerous questions about how life seem "unfair" to others, I would end this book with thousands of pages. But let me tell you that life is fair. God has a perfect plan for everyone. Only trust in the Lord knowing only God can do.

Of course, there are hundreds of books that suggest ways to overcome challenges in life. God bless such authors. All these books are good—they help us discipline ourselves to reach our goals. But for fulfilling life's purpose and overcoming life's challenges, the Christian needs the total dependence on God. And it is never too late to make changes necessary to have a successful life. Only depend on God and His mighty power. Dependence is an expression of faith. In who? In God. Put your trust in God alone! For, He alone has good plans for your life. His plan is to make you prosper.

"It is God who directs the lives of His creatures; everyone's life is in His power" (according to Job 12:10 GNT). God's plans for you are extraordinary: To make you smile and to turn your life around. You must trust God that He is your only source of life and happiness. Patience is a virtue to success. Remember that you exist because of God's hedge of protection, mercy and favour. The psalmist says, "Because He lives I can face tomorrow." Truly, without God, life ceases to exist.

The question still remains: "In our world of pain, where is God?" Some people cannot comprehend the existence of a God who would allow such misery. But no one can question the prerogative of God. God said to His servant Job, "Where were you when I laid the earth's foundation? Tell me, if you understand. Who marked off its dimensions?" (Job 38:4–5). From the statement, we can infer of God's creative power, the depth of His wisdom, and His unsearchable knowledge. Can we leave God behind because things are rough?

I don't think to have answers about life. I have a book called the Bible. All the important questions of life are answered in the Bible. I've studied the Bible, and I can enumerate some of the reasons we often go through difficulties. I advise you to start studying the Bible, and God will help you find answers to numerous questions as well. In addition, there are a lot of Bible characters who went through tough times, and God rescued them. Their stories are great lessons to us— they will help us know what to do in times of need.

In this chapter, three Bible stories are discussed, and they are stories of people who were able to overcome life challenges: The stories of Job, Paul and Silas, and Hannah, the mother of Samuel.

Job is the hero of the book that bears his name. Originally, he is from Uz, probably in northern Arabia. He is thus apparently a non-Jew. Neither his wife nor his original ten children are named in the book of Job.

The book of Job discusses one theological issue, the question of suffering. There are nine groups of participants in this story: Job, the four friends, Job's wife, Job's children, the four messengers, Satan, sons of God, God, and the narrator.

In the first part of the narrative framework, Job is introduced as a perfect and pious person, and wealthy as well. He has a large family: A wife, three daughters who live in their father's big house, and seven sons who all have their own apartments, where they continuously host extravagant celebrations for their siblings.

The second scene shifts to the divine council, the gathering of "the children of God" and Satan also presents himself at their meeting. God asks Satan his mission and starts proceedings by questioning him about Job. Satan's observation that Job's piety is linked to his prosperity is made known to God, and he challenges God to strike His servant Job down and see the consequences of his actions, if he will not curse Him. Finally, God delivers Job into the hands of Satan.

The third scene returns to Job. His children are in their oldest brother's house, as usual. As they host their celebration, four messengers in succession describe the loss of Job's livestock (his sheep, his oxen, and his camels) and the obliteration of his children.

The fourth scene is about Job's prayer. It is a prayer of intercession; he prays constantly for his children during their celebration. Maybe his children say something against God, and he stands on their behalf for pardon, so that God will forgive them. Job's intercession tells us how prayerful and upright he is. In addition, his life sums up the godly parent he is and shows that he is willing to allow God to rule in his family.

The fifth scene is Job's reaction after receiving the bad news: He starts praising God. Job's praise is recorded in Job 1:20–22: "Naked I came from my mother's womb, and naked I will depart. The Lord gave and the Lord has taken away; may the name of the Lord be praised. In all this, Job did not sin by charging God with wrongdoing." Job's faithfulness to God endures.

Sixth, Job's wife, whose name is unknown, tried to persuade her husband to curse God for the trouble He (God) has caused him. All her attempts amount to failure. Job does not listen to his wife; he trusts God, in times of trouble, that He is faithful. Listen to Job's reply to his wife: "You are talking like a foolish woman. Shall we accept good from God, and not trouble?" (Job 2:10)

Seventh, the three friends of Job, Eliphaz the Temanite, Bilhad the Shuhite, and Zophar the Naamathite, sympathise with Job. These friends rehearse the cliché of tradition: God rewards goodness and punishes wickedness. And so if Job is suffering, he deserves it. Finally, they plead with Job to confess his sins and ask God for pardon, and his troubles will cease.

Finally, Job challenges God to explain why this trouble has happened to him. But God does not speak to Job (Read chapters 38–41). The episode ends with the Lord rebuking the three friends for not giving good advice and restoring Job's wealth, including all his children. The fourth friend, Eliud, is not rebuked (chapters 32–37).

In this episode, God sets things right to prove Satan wrong that, Job is not righteous just because he is being blessed. Job lost everything (children and wealth), but he did not lose his faith in his God. Job suffered unjustly, yet he did not blame God for his sufferings. No Christian is insulated from suffering.

God does not tempt us (James 1:13). When we are tempted by the Devil, our faith, our patience, our self-control, our endurance, and our love for God are put to test. How can we see the gracious hand of God if we never go into temptations? Again, how can we see the wonders of God that our forefathers have been talking about when we never face life's challenges?

This episode also teaches us about the kind of friends we need in our lives. Job's friends tried to console him but they soon started to blame him for his own troubles, inferring that he must have sinned in order for all the troubles to come upon him. This same incidence occurred during Jesus's ministry: His disciples asked Him after healing a blind man from birth, "Rabbi, who sinned, this man or his parents, that he was born blind?" (John 9:2). Jesus answered them, "Neither this man nor his parents sinned, but this happened so that the works of God might be displayed in him" (verse 3).

Job's episode, together with other events educates us that suffering is not always a result of sin. As long as we remain Christians, suffering is bound to come our way. Besides, as long as we live as humans, sickness is inevitable—headache, fever, diabetes, cancer, stroke, miscarriage and so on. Bear in mind that not all circumstances are embedded with spiritual implications.

Last, we learn from Job's episode that, in times of suffering, we can still serve God. Apostle Paul asks: "Can anything ever separate us from Christ's love? Does it mean he no longer loves us if we have trouble or calamity, or are persecuted, or hungry, or threatened with death?" (Romans 8:35 NLT). In verse 39, he says, "Nothing in all creation will ever separate us from the love of God that is revealed in Christ Jesus our Lord."

The second story is about **Paul and Silas (Acts 16:16-40)** who went to jail because of the gospel. These two missionaries travelled all over, walking and preaching. Some of these people were happy to listen to the good news about Christ, but others were unhappy and angry to hear them speak about Christ. But these two men continued to preach the gospel.

Preaching the Gospel of the Kingdom of God has never been easy. We live in a world which hates the truth. People could kill the innocent and still have lawyers to defend them in our courtrooms. In many countries for examples, it could cost your life to stand for the truth. Needless to say, most of our Judges, politicians and law enforcement agents are dishonest leaders in the nation. Can we trust our pastors? Yes, we can. There are faithful men of God among us. Yet there are a lot of false prophets out there. Be careful that you're not deceived by them. Take note of what Jesus tells His disciples "By their fruits you will recognise them" (Matthew 7:16). In conclusion, let us bear in mind that the Christian has no option but to stand for the truth.

The story unfolds that one day a man got very angry at what Paul and Silas were telling the people and had them beaten, arrested, and put in prison. The jailer was told if these men (Paul and Silas) escaped, he would be killed. So he locked their feet with stocks so that these they could not escape from the prison.

This story is so remarkable because it teaches the Christian about having faith in God no matter the situation one finds himself or herself in. At the end, God is there as a rescuer.

They prayed to God because they loved Him and knew He was their rescuer. And all the prisoners could hear them praising and worshipping God. It's a beautiful story because it teaches us that we can still praise God in our sufferings.

Surprisingly, the jailer fell asleep. All of a sudden, there was an earthquake, and the chains fell off their feet, they were freed, and the doors of the prison opened. What's more is that when the jailer woke from his sleep and held out his sword to stab himself, Paul and Silas said to him, "We didn't run away; don't kill yourself." The jailer was surprised to see them not trying to escape from the prison. Finally, the jailer didn't kill himself, and they thanked God the more.

From the story, we learn that Paul and Silas went to prison because of the good news about Christ. Introducing Jesus into the lives of others shouldn't have been a problem; but rather a glad tiding to all people. However, men who live in sin find it extremely difficult to welcome Christ into their lives because they see Him as a threat to their wicked ways. Christ's life is far opposite to that of the worldly man. He is holy; humble; faithful; good; and loving. Whereas, those living in sin are unholy; proud; unfaithful; wicked; and mean. The Bible says, "Everyone who does evil hates the light, and will not come into the light for fear that his deeds will be exposed" (John 3:20).

Have you ever heard of a preacher or a missionary who had been falsely accused or maltreated or imprisoned because of the Gospel? Jesus said, "If the world hates you, keep in mind that it hated me first. If you belonged to the world, it would love you as its own. As it is, you do not belong to the world, but I have chosen you out of the world. That is why the world hates you" (John 15:18).

The Christian should bear in mind that God has every means to help us in times of need. In the case of Paul and Silas, God used something very dramatic to deliver them: An earthquake. What is so amazing in this story is that the earthquake did not have a destructive purpose: It was constructive.

In this episode, we learn that God freed Paul and Silas from the shackles of their feet, and finally these two missionaries were out of prison. Their intentions were good—to preach the Gospel of Christ to sinners—this shouldn't have been a problem to the inhabitants of the city. However, they were caught up in a big trouble by going to jail.

The story also teaches us that no matter how good we are, sufferings can come our way, and when they come, God is there as a rescuer. At the end of everything, the prison guard witnessed how God is able to save His people in times of suffering. Always know that

God is with you wherever you go—God's promise is well spelled out: "I am with you always, even to the end of age" (Matthew 28:20). Just as He "fought" for Paul and Silas, so will He fight your battles for you.

The third story is about **Hannah**. The book of First Samuel contains the story of this God-fearing woman. Who is this Hannah, and what does the story have to offer? We know Hannah for her sorrow. But her conduct during her time of sorrow teaches the Christian, especially women to pray in times of need. But the sad news is that, most women would visit false prophets who would tell them what their itching ears would want to hear. At the end, they are deceived. Hannah would advise you to go on your knees and pray to your Father Who is in heaven. Hannah is a woman of faith for women in our generation. As a woman, how often do you pray?

Who is Hannah? Hannah was the wife of Elkanah. Elkanah had two wives, namely Hannah and Peninnah. Hannah was his first wife, and Peninnah was his second wife. Peninnah had children, but Hannah had no children. Because of this, Hannah was very grieved. Hannah desperately desired a child but was unable to conceive. To make the matter worse, Peninnah taunted Hannah concerning her barrenness. But Elkanah was kind to Hannah.

The story is full of wisdom applications in that Hannah cried out to God about her situation. Who do you pray to when life seems insurmountable to you? James asks, "Is anyone among you in trouble?" and answers by saying, "Let them pray" (James 5:13).

Prayer causes God's attention (1 Peter 3:12). Prayer is the key to our problems. Prayer is you talking with God. It is an intimate link that keeps a Christian in constant contact with the heavenly Father just like a person-to-person phone call. Prayer is a cry. Just as little children cry to their mothers, the same way you should cry to God. When you pray according to the will of God, He answers your prayer. Jesus said to His disciples, "When you pray, say 'Our Father in heaven, hallowed be your name'" (Matthew 6:9). God is our Father, and as a Father, He is ever ready to listen to us when we need Him. Jesus says, "If you evil men know how to give good things to your children, how much more will your heavenly Father, who is in heaven, not give good things to those who ask Him" (Matthew 15:9). From this account, Jesus tells us that the Father is ever ready to give good things to all His children. Are you a child of God? If yes, "Ask, and it shall be given to you; seek, and you shall find; knock, and the door shall be opened unto you" (Matthew 7:7).

In scripture, we read of kings, prophets, and ordinary people like you and me, who averted destruction by praying. Joshua prayed to stop the sun (Joshua 10:3), one prayed for fire to come down from heaven (2 Kings 1:12), and one gained an additional fifteen years to his life by praying (2 Kings 18:5; Isaiah 38:5). All these Bible characters prayed intensely to God.

Where is this God Who answers prayers? He is not a dead God; He is alive! When you are in need, pray to God, and He will listen to you. In the case of Hannah, she did what was right—she prayed! She promised the Lord that if He would give her a son, she would dedicate him to serve God as a Nazarite (a man set apart to serve God; Numbers 6:1–8).

Finally, the Lord answered Hannah's prayer. She gave birth to a son and named him Samuel, whose name means "asked of God." The story unfolds that when the child was old enough, Hannah kept her promise to the Lord, taking little Samuel to Eli, and giving him to the Lord to serve in God's tabernacle.

Hannah's thanksgiving is recorded in 1 Samuel 2:2: "There is no one holy like the Lord; there is no one besides you; there is no Rock like our God." In her worship, God is presented as the Lord of all.

The end of story is the statement below: "The greatest miracle God ever performed was allowing Jesus to die for our sins. Is there anything too hard for Him? The answer is no. God knows our challenges—the pains, the humiliations, the sicknesses, and the persecutions we encounter in our daily life. The secret of contentment in life is having Christ, because He is the only One Who gives life, and the life He gives is eternal. Those who are very much content in life are able to give themselves freely, and that is God's requirement for living in Him. Those who have found Jesus have found peace." Amen!

Conclusion of *Fragments: God Loves Everyone.*

Certainly, God will make all things new simply because the planet earth is heavily polluted and clothed with lots of sins, such that a new earth should be created for its replacement. The magnitude of sin on earth is such that God could not tolerate the gravity of our sinful nature anymore.

Notwithstanding the enormity of humanity's sin, God continues to love humanity in a grand style. That God loves everyone has been exponentially expanded in fragments in this piece of writing and cannot be underestimated. From the perspective of reading *Fragments*, it is realised that the theme of love is the *primus inter pares* among billions of God's attributes. Indeed, the love of God expanded to humankind is immeasurable. There is no occasion whatsoever when God has withdrawn His love for human beings.

When our first parents sinned, God, in His infinite love, made a plan of salvation for humanity. Christ came to the earth to save the lost. His coming to save humankind is through the instrumentality of God. And it is always said in scriptures that "God so loved the world that he gave his one and only Son, that whoever believes in him shall not perish but have eternal life" (John 3:16).

Jesus was used as ransom for forgiveness of humanity's sins. The cross, of course, is what it took. The cross does not save; Jesus saves! A Bible teacher once said, "There were many people at the feet of the cross while Jesus was there, but they were not saved." Looking on to Jesus, Who was crucified on the cross, and believing in Him that He is your Saviour, you will be saved.

As Christians, we are God's agents to bring hope to the hopeless, to show that there is a God Who loves and cares for them. The apostle Paul was a key leader in acting on this revelation. His calling from God made him the right person to guide the church into new era of mission to all people. As God did not intend to limit His salvation to only His chosen people, the Israelites, Jonah was sent as a missionary by God to the Gentiles so that they could hear the word of God, repent, and be saved.

In addition to the above, God was able to use His power through various ordeals, such as a fiery furnace and a den of lions, to carry His message into a pagan land. Daniel and his company, John the Baptist, Peter, and many more served as missionaries for the spread of the Gospel.

As it has been observed, God uses people to bring His word to others. Today, there are millions of Christian disciples who are spreading the Gospel of Christ to others. The crucial point to remember is that Jesus has revealed to us the character of God, and this tells us a lot about God's love for humanity and His desire for as many as possible to be saved. In addition to our salvation, Jesus promises us heaven: "Do not let your heart be troubled. Trust in God, trust also in me. In my Father's house are many rooms, if it were not so, I would have told you. I am going there to prepare a place for you" (Matthew 14:1, 2).

We have also learned that Christ is the centre of the Gospel. Whenever we decide to preach the Gospel of the Kingdom of God, there is only one name that should be on our minds and lips, and that name is Jesus.

As Christians, it is our moral duty to go to the hopeless and get them informed that God cares for them irrespective of the magnitude of their sins. The only thing for them to do is to believe in Christ.

Finding a Church.

Now, after believing in Christ, the next step is to find a church where you adhere to and can feel at home. The church is a place we go to worship God. One may ask, "But can't we worship God anywhere we are located?" Of course, we can! We can worship God wherever we are. It is God's command that we Christians find ourselves together as one body in Christ (Hebrews 10:25).

Think of it like this. Can we have a farmer without a farm, or a teacher without students? The answer is no. Likewise, you cannot be a Christian without belonging to a church, marry and still remain single, or play music without sound. When the sinner comes to Christ, he or she becomes a child of God, and thereafter enters into the family of God and belongs to the "household of faith" (See Galatians 6:10).

The church is a place where one can encounter oneself together with other Christian believers. In church, you get to know other Christians who will be able to encourage you in your new faith in Christ Jesus. During preaching, teachings, testimonies, worship, and praises, the Christian is edified. In church, you can hear sound teachings from the Bible that will help you acquire knowledge about the things of God.

Now, try to find a church where you can belong. There are so many churches, and you may wonder which of the churches you should adhere to. Choose a church where Christ is highly lifted, a church where sin is easily condemned, and a church where its focus is on discipleship. In addition, you need a church where the people are friendly. For this reason, you should take your time looking for a church. Visit a few church services before you finally decide where you will belong to.

Finally, get yourself a copy of the Bible. If you don't have money to buy one, you can go to any nearby church, ask to speak to the pastor, tell him or her about your new faith, and finally ask to be given a copy of the Bible. After receiving the Bible, begin to study it every day to learn more about Jesus and His Word. You can begin your studies with the Gospel according to John. It is believed that as time goes on, you will begin to have new knowledge about God and the things of God. But the most important aspect of your Bible studies is not just to acquire godly knowledge, but also to abide in it. John 15:4 says, "If you abide in me and my words abide in you, you will ask of anything, and it shall be given unto you." Samuel said to King Saul, "Obedience is better than sacrifice" (1 Samuel 15:22).

Different Temperaments in Churches.

Now, you need to understand that the church is a collection of people from different cultural or tribal groups. As they walk together, values sometimes conflict. The Church is also a place where people have gone through series of sufferings before meeting Jesus, Who is now their source of hope and strength. Let anyone who come to Jesus the Saviour know that, we don't come to Jesus with our better lives; we come to Jesus with our miserable lives for transformation.

Human Behaviour Study identifies four basic personality types: Sanguine, choleric, melancholic, and phlegmatic. Being cognizant of this, the sinner, who is now a Christian, should know that the church could be filled with individuals who are troublemakers, unforgiving, mean and cantankerous—they are all God's children who need transformation.

What advice do you give to the one who is already a member in the church? How do you treat those who join the church for the first time? Do you treat them good in order for them to stay, or you treat them bad so that they leave the church? The simple advice is: Your new faith in Christ should produce good fruit so that others may see Christ in you.

The new convert should also know that not all people who are found in church are Christians. There are people who go to church whenever they wish; church does not become a priority to them. Others attend church because of friends. There are still others who go with the intention of causing divisions, and those who are there to cause others to sin. The question is, "What are your motives for following Christ?"

One important thing to know is that we respond to Christ's invitation, and not humankind's invitation. We need to keep our eyes on Jesus. Don't leave the church because someone offended you. On the other hand, old convert Christians are advised to be kind to new convert Christians, who have come to worship God with us. We should pray for them that they will continually stay at the feet of Christ. The end of the matter is that we should let our new converts feel at home.

A Word of Advice.

We end this book with an invitation to a new beginning with Christ. Much has been said about Christ: His death on the cross, His forgiveness of sins, and His free gift of eternal life. Finally, His promise of heaven to born-again Christians who would be faithful to the end, is an extra package. Today is a new commitment. Open up your heart to Jesus.

Dear one, I strongly believe this book points you to Christ. Honestly speaking, I have had the priviledge to talk with people from all sorts of religious groups; I have walked and passionately shared Christ with hundreds of them; but I never preached about religion and my church. I did not talk about any other person except Christ, Who came down from heaven to die for the sins of humanity. I believe church and religion do not save. And there is no other person who is able to give us life. Only Jesus saves! Look to Jesus and live.

PRAYER OF SALVATION:

Dear God, I realise that I am a sinner. I also realise that Jesus died for my sins. I am sorry and I ask You to forgive me. I now give my life to You: Come into my life and save me. I give You control of my life and I ask that You would rule and reign in my life so that Your perfect will would be accomplished in my life. Amen!

DATE:

Made in the USA
Columbia, SC
03 April 2018